DIVIDING
THE
EARTH!

Noah's Legacy

WHO OWNS RIGHTS TO THE LAND?

Cassius V. Stuart

This publication contains the opinions and ideas of its author. It is intended to provide helpful and informative material on the subject matter covered. It is sold with the understanding that the author and publisher are not engaged in rendering professional service in the book. If the reader requires professional assistance or advice, a competent professional should be consulted.

The author and the publisher expressly disclaim any responsibility for any liability, loss, or risk, personnel or otherwise, which is incurred as a consequence, directly or indirectly, of the use and application of any of the content of this book.

DIVIDING
THE
EARTH!

Noah's Legacy

WHO OWNS RIGHTS TO THE LAND?

DEDICATION

To the unyielding quest for Peace

"Dividing the Earth: Noah's Legacy" is not just a testament to historical tales and covenants made; it stands as a beacon, reminding us of our shared origins and the intertwined destinies that beckon us toward peace. To every soul who has yearned for peace amidst turmoil and for those who have laid down their differences in the cause of unity, this book is dedicated. May its pages inspire a future where divisions fade, and the bonds of brotherhood prevail, echoing the true legacy of our forebears.

ACKNOWLEDGMENTS

First and foremost, I'd like to extend my deepest gratitude to my family. Your unwavering support and faith in me have been the bedrock upon which this work stands. Your patience, encouragement, and belief in the importance of this narrative have been instrumental in bringing "Dividing the Earth: Noah's Legacy" to fruition.

This book does not aim to prescribe solutions to the complex crisis in the Middle East, a region with deeply interwoven histories and passions. Instead, it seeks to delve into the very origins of the issues, tracing back to an oath taken eons ago. By understanding our shared past, we hope to shed light on present-day intricacies.

To all who have lent their insights, shared their perspectives, and contributed in myriad ways to this project, your voices have been invaluable. Every conversation and every shared piece of wisdom have enriched this journey of exploration and discovery.

Lastly, to every reader who picks up this book: may you find clarity, understanding, and perhaps a renewed hope for the future. Together, by acknowledging our roots, we can foster a deeper understanding of the paths that lie ahead.

With gratitude,
Cassius V Stuart

TABLE OF CONTENTS

∽⌐∾

Introduction   13

Chapter 1   15

    The Flood   15

    The Post-Flood World: 16

The Geographical Challenge & Diverse Landscape   16

    Surveying the Transformed World: 16

    The Challenges Ahead: 18

The Divine Command   19

    Noah's Revelatory Moment with the Divine: 19

    Noah's Moment of Uncertainty: 21

    The significance of the Task: 22

Chapter 2   23

Noah divided the Earth   23

    In the Modern-Day Bible: 23

    From the Book of Jasher: 24

    The Detailed Account from the Book"of J'bilees: 25

Chapter 3   27

How was the Earth Divided   27

Ham's Inheritance   27

    The Land of Africa   27

Japheth's Inheritance: The Expanses of North Asia,
Europe, and the Five Prominent Isles   28
The Sacred Inheritance of Shem:
Middle East, India, and China   30
The Middle East: The Cradle of Civilization   30
India: A Rich Heritage of Spirituality   30
China: Ancient Wisdom and Civilization   31
Noah's Rejoice and Prophecy   31
Noah's Blessing as a Continuing Legacy   32
The Dead Sea Scrolls   33

Chapter 4   35
The Land of Many Names.   35
The Genealogy of Japheth   38
The Genealogy of Ham   40
The Genealogy from Shem to Abraham   43
The Genealogy from Abraham to Israel   46

Chapter 5   49
Linking the Dots.   49
The Sacred Blessing   50
Oath and Covenant   52
Violation of the oath   55

Chapter 6   59
Abraham's Promise   59
The Promise of Land: 59
The Significance of Shem: 60
God's Respect for Boundaries: 61
Joshua and the Canaanites   62
Fulfillment of God's Promise: 66

The Book of Jubilees and the Divine Mandate:　67

The Oath and Divine Reckoning:　67

The Oath and Divine Reckoning:　68

The Exile to the Return　68

From the Romans to 1948, the state of Israel　71

The Second Exile and Return: From Roman

Destruction to the Establishment of the State of Israel　71

The Great Revolt (66-70 AD):　71

Destruction of the Second Temple (70 AD):　72

The Diaspora:　73

Bar Kokhba Revolt (132-135 AD):　73

Diaspora Life:　74

The Oath and the Jewish Diaspora:

Exploring Historical Linkages　76

The Oath:　76

Persecution in Europe:　77

Counterarguments:　77

The Hope of Returning Home　78

Prophecy Fulfilled:

The Zionist Movement and the Return　81

Birth of Zionism:　82

From the Birth of Zionism to the Balfour Declaration:　83

The Emergence of Modern Zionism:　83

Diplomatic Efforts:　84

World War I and the Ottoman Empire:　84

Britain's Strategic Interests:　84

The Balfour Declaration:　84

The British Mandate of Palestine (1920-1948):

A Period of Transition and Tumult　85

Establishing the Mandate: 85

Jewish Immigration and Settlement: 86

Arab Concerns and Opposition: 86

British Policy and the White Papers: 86

World War II and its Aftermath: 87

The Road to Partition: 87

End of the Mandate and Birth of Israel: 87

Establishment of the State of Israel: 88

Chapter 7 93

Benjamin and the Palestinian People 93

Origin of the Palestinian People 94

The Ottoman Empire and the Arab Settlement in Palestine 95

Binding oath 97

Reflections 100

Bibliography 103

INTRODUCTION

∽o∾

In the dawn of human history, as ancient texts recount, the patriarch Noah apportioned the world among his three sons: Shem, Ham, and Japheth. This division was more than just a land allotment; it set the groundwork for future genealogies and civilizations. Using these ancient texts as a guide, we delve into the intricate accounts of these partitions, unveiling the vast territories inherited by each son. From the peaks of Râfā to the shores of the Egyptian Sea and from the fiery mountains of Africa to the vast terrains of Asia, these land grants significantly influenced the spread and establishment of nations. Along with these territorial delineations, the narrative intertwines prophecies, blessings, and curses. These divisions, along with the blessings and subsequent misdeeds, especially by Canaan, have underpinned centuries of history, warfare, and cultural evolution. This book sheds light on these ancient partitions, spotlighting an era where divine will and human aspirations merged to mold the world's geographical and spiritual topography.

Over time, the divisions in ancient texts have spurred both marvels and miseries. Throughout millennia, territories assigned to Shem, Ham, and Japheth's descendants have seen civilizations at their pinnacle, as well as significant discord and battles. With the passage of centuries, some of these territorial demarcations merged, giving birth to mighty empires, from the Mesopotamians and Persians to the Romans and Ottomans.

Among these divisions, one of the most enduring and contentious legacies is the struggle over the Levantine territory, particularly between the Jews, descendants of Shem, and the Canaanites, descendants of Ham. Over the ages, the scattered Jewish communities, following periods of persecution and exile, yearned for their ancestral lands. The Zionist movement encapsulated this sentiment in the late 19th and early 20th centuries. Yet, their hopes frequently collided with those of the region's Arab residents, leading to numerous confrontations and wars.

The establishment of Israel in 1948 became a defining juncture in this narrative. The land, revered by both Jews and Palestinians, turned into a flashpoint of profound discord. Despite numerous peace endeavors, from the Oslo to the Abraham Accords, central challenges persist. The unresolved question looms: Who truly has the right to this land? Palestinian aspirations for sovereignty and the refugees' right to return remain juxtaposed against Israel's security needs and deep-rooted historical and spiritual ties.

Presently, escalating tensions in Gaza and the West Bank have culminated in a full-scale war declared by Israel as a result of a terrorist attack by Hamas militants on Israeli civilians. This book seeks to navigate the annals of history, striving to uncover the authentic custodians of the territory now named Palestine and to fathom why, for millennia, blood has been spilled over this land.

CHAPTER 1

The Flood

While many people think of the Middle East crisis as a recent challenge, it has deep historical roots going back thousands of years. This complex issue can be traced to events over 4,500 years ago. One of the significant moments from this time was the Great Flood. As the massive floodwaters began to recede, Noah and his family stepped out from the Ark, which had been their refuge. They were the sole survivors in a world that a catastrophic deluge had completely transformed.

This post-flood world was a mix of wonder and devastation. As they explored, they saw lands that bore signs of nature's fury and divine intervention. These lands were not just a reminder of the flood but also symbolized God's might and mercy.

Through this story, we learn more about Noah, who is portrayed as a beacon of hope and unwavering faith. He and his descendants had to navigate a dramatically altered world, facing challenges and changes that were, in many ways, unprecedented in human history. Their journey highlights the resilience and adaptability of humanity in the face of immense adversity.

The Post-Flood World:

After the great flood, when Noah's family stepped out of the ark, they encountered a world vastly different from what they remembered. They found themselves on Mount Ararat, situated in what we now know as eastern Turkey, near the borders of both Armenia and Iran. As they looked around, the landscape was filled with waterlogged areas, remnants of the massive flood, and subtle hints of what the land used to be.

In this new world, the effects of the flood were evident everywhere. Vast stretches of land were soaked, and the aftermath of the deluge was visible. Amidst the desolation, however, there were signs of life beginning anew. Small plants were starting to grow, animals were venturing out, and the world was slowly showing signs of recovery.

For Noah and his family, this presented a unique challenge. Not only did they have to navigate the emotional weight of surviving such a catastrophic event, but they also had the monumental task of rebuilding human civilization. They had to start from scratch – finding shelter, sourcing food, and re-establishing a community. The narrative paints a vivid picture of their resilience, determination, and faith as they embarked on this journey of rebuilding a world forever changed by the flood.

THE GEOGRAPHICAL
CHALLENGE & DIVERSE LANDSCAPE

Surveying the Transformed World:

Noah and his family embark on a monumental mission to survey the newly reshaped world, a landscape forever altered by the

Great Flood. As they journey through this unfamiliar terrain, they encounter many geographical challenges, each presenting unique obstacles and opportunities.

Barren Wastelands: Much of the world is marked by barren wastelands—stretches of desolation where the floodwaters have left their mark. These areas lack vegetation and habitable resources, presenting a stark and unforgiving landscape. Noah and his family must navigate these wastelands, seeking signs of life and sustenance.

Rugged Mountain Ranges: In their exploration, they come across rugged mountain ranges, towering remnants of the pre-Flood world. These peaks present both challenges and advantages. While they offer vantage points for surveying the land, they also pose treacherous climbs and unpredictable weather patterns that can test their resilience.

Vast Waterlogged Plains: The floodwaters have left vast, waterlogged plains in their wake. These expansive, marshy areas present challenges in terms of mobility and settlement. Noah's family must find ways to traverse these waters while searching for stable ground to establish their new home.

The Promise of Fertile Valleys: Amidst the desolation, they discover pockets of fertile valleys. These oases offer hope and sustenance, teeming with plant life and potential agricultural resources. Here, they can envision building a future for themselves and their descendants.

Coastal Regions and Rivers: Coastal regions and riverbanks provide access to water and potential trade routes. These areas hold the promise of fish and other aquatic resources vital for sustenance. However, they also bring the challenge of unpredictable tides and the need to adapt to coastal living.

Diverse Climates: The world's climates have shifted, creating a diverse range of environments, from arid deserts to temperate forests. Each climate zone presents unique opportunities and challenges, influencing the types of flora and fauna that can be found and the strategies needed for survival.

As readers journey alongside Noah and his family through these diverse landscapes, they gain insight into the resilience of the human spirit and the capacity to adapt in the face of adversity. The geographical challenges become a metaphor for life's unpredictability, requiring resourcefulness, cooperation, and faith to overcome. This exploration of the reshaped world serves as a backdrop to the larger narrative, where Noah's family grapples not only with physical challenges but also with moral and spiritual decisions as they fulfill their divine mission.

The Challenges Ahead:

As they took on the challenge of replenishing the earth, everywhere they looked, they saw signs of the flood's power, turning once familiar places into unfamiliar terrains. As they stepped out of the Ark, the vastness of their responsibility became clear. They were the only survivors, and restarting life on Earth rested on their shoulders.

Building new homes for their families became their immediate concern. The land was different, sometimes muddy and unstable, making their journey challenging. They had to use their memories of the old world and their resourcefulness to find or create safe spots to camp and build new communities.

But beyond the physical tasks, they also faced a profound spiritual responsibility. God's initial instructions to Adam to grow the population and care for the Earth was now their mission. Noah's three sons – Shem, Ham, and Japheth – were to be the heads of new families, spreading out and populating different regions. They needed to make wise decisions, thinking about the future generations that would come from them.

As days turned into weeks and weeks into months, they encountered various challenges. There were disputes about land and resources and sometimes doubts about their mission. But throughout their journey, there were moments of hope and joy, where they celebrated small victories and witnessed the world's rebirth.

The story of Noah and his family is not just about survival but about faith, determination, and the human spirit's ability to endure and rebuild. It showcases how, even in the most trying times, people can come together, guided by a higher purpose, and create a new beginning.

THE DIVINE COMMAND

Noah's Revelatory Moment with the Divine:
Several generations had passed since Noah's ark came to rest upon the mountains of Ararat. During that time, his descendants had multiplied abundantly, spreading across the earth like stars in the night sky. This increase brought with it a growing contention over the sprawling terrains that lay untouched and ripe for the taking.

Brothers and their families, once unified by the trials of the flood, now found themselves at odds, their bonds strained by the desire to claim and cultivate their own pieces of the world.

It was in the days of **Peleg** that a profound transformation took place, mirroring the divisions among Noah's descendants. Two pivotal events occurred: the division of the vast land that was their inheritance, and a dramatic ideological shift that would have lasting repercussions on human history. This shift was not rooted in a mere disagreement over boundaries or kinship—it originated from the collective ambition of humanity embodied in the construction of the Tower of Babel. Their goal was singular and audacious: to build a tower that would reach the heavens, a testament to their own greatness and unity. However, this act of pride prompted God's intervention that confused their language. Communication collapsed, and the once unified people were now divided by the varied tongues that arose from this event. Discord spread as the people, unable to understand one another, were scattered across the earth, taking with them the diverse languages that marked the beginnings of separate nations and cultures.

From this chaos, the people were scattered in all directions, driven as much by misunderstanding as by the divine will of God that stirred the air and twisted their tongues. They carried with them the embryonic essence of future nations, cultures that would take root in distant lands, each marked by a distinct language that would define their identity. The Tower of Babel was not just a symbol of mankind's Haughtiness; it was the birthplace of a multitude of dialects, each carrying the legacy of that division, etching the story of humanity's divergence across the earth.

Amid this upheaval, a pivotal event unfolded. Noah, whose faith had been demonstrated in the salvation of his family through the building of the Ark, felt the stirrings of God once again. In a conversation that transcended the ordinary, God presented a directive of immense consequence. This discourse, filled with destiny and guidance, recognized Noah's unwavering commitment and entrusted him with a grave responsibility. The new world, still fresh and malleable from the remnants of the great deluge, was to be divided among his three sons: Shem, Ham, and Japheth.

This division was not solely of land but of legacy. Each son was tasked with leading his descendants to different corners of the globe, sowing the seeds of new settlements and cultivating distinct cultures and beliefs. From these seeds would grow countless civilizations, each with unique traditions and histories that would stretch across the ages. The trust placed in Noah was monumental, marking a decisive moment that would shape the fabric of human history. The decisions made and the boundaries drawn would resonate through time, as humanity's narrative unfolded from the groundwork established by Noah and the ensuing journey of his descendants.

Noah's Moment of Uncertainty:

Upon receiving God's directive, Noah is flooded with emotions and uncertainty. The immense responsibility of dividing the rejuvenated world among his three sons is no small feat. Every inch of the new landscape has its own character and potential, making it even more challenging to decide who gets what. He's torn between God's command and ensuring fairness to his sons. As a leader, he knows that the decisions he makes now will shape the future of humanity.

Being a father adds another layer to his dilemma. He wants to ensure that each of his sons feels valued and has an equal chance to thrive. The weight of these considerations presses on him. After much contemplation, Noah recalls an ancient tradition of drawing lots—a method seen as unbiased and leaving the outcome to divine will. Using this approach, he hopes to bring fairness to his sons and obedience to God's command, ensuring a harmonious future for future generations.

The significance of the Task:

Noah's challenge wasn't just about dividing up a piece of land; it was much more than that. It was about envisioning and setting the foundation for what would become entire nations, each with its distinct culture, traditions, and languages. This task, set upon him by God, emphasized the profound bond between the Creator and creation.

God's directive wasn't merely a set of instructions; it was a testament to the idea that humans were chosen to shape the world's destiny. And Noah, despite the enormity of the task and the potential doubts that might plague anyone in his shoes, remained steadfast. His unwavering faith in God and commitment to the divine mission are lessons in trust, resilience, and determination

The saga of Noah is more than just a biblical story; it's a lesson on the limitless power of faith, the courage required to embrace the unknown, and the importance of being aligned with a purpose that transcends oneself. It underscores the idea that, even amidst uncertainty and doubts, with conviction and trust in a higher power, humans have the potential to shape history.

CHAPTER 2

ᕫᕤᕫ

"And as the thirty-third jubilee dawned, the Earth was divided into three portions, each to be inherited by Shem, Ham, and Japheth."
Jubilees

NOAH DIVIDED THE EARTH

In the Modern-Day Bible:

The growth of humanity across the vast expanses of Earth necessitated a division of the land, and the ancient texts guided how this was to be done. In my quarter-century of studying the Scriptures one enigmatic statement in **Genesis 10:25** has consistently intrigued and puzzled me. It's a fleeting reference, a mere whisper in the grand tapestry of biblical narratives. The verse reads, "Two sons were born to Heber: One was named Peleg, for in his time the earth was divided; his brother was named Joktan."

For something so important as this, the brevity of the statement stands out, especially in a world where detailed explanations are the norm. This succinctness leaves many, including myself, in a state of perplexity, yearning for more insight. What does it truly signify for the earth to be "divided"? Is this referring to a geological split, a division of political territories, or perhaps something of a deeper, more profound nature? The abrupt nature of this verse, lacking any substantial context, presents itself almost like a solitary puzzle piece, seemingly disconnected from the greater narrative.

Modern interpretations of the Bible, aimed at appealing to today's audience, often maintain simplified narratives. These versions tend to provide just a cursory overview of events, lacking in-depth exploration. This approach, while perhaps more digestible, risks omitting the nuanced details and richness that truly define these historical events. Consequently, this leaves scholars, readers, and contemporary society with a significant gap in understanding historical events that continue to influence many today. Such a gap underscores the importance of delving deeper into these texts to grasp the full scope and impact of these ancient stories.

Genesis 10:25 serves as a poignant example of this. While it hints at a pivotal moment in human history, its concise nature leaves so much unsaid. For scholars, such verses become starting points for deeper exploration. They summon us to delve into the recesses of history, archaeology, and theology to unearth the deeper truths concealed within. In this journey of exploration, we are reminded that every word, no matter how briefly mentioned, holds significance and invites us to unlock its mysteries.

From the Book of Jasher:
The modern Bible and the Book of Jasher[1] touch upon a significant event: the division of the Earth after the Tower of Babel's construction. This narrative, while summarized in the Bible, is delved into greater detail in the Book of Jasher, Chapter 7.

---

1   The Book of Jasher is referenced in Joshua 10:3 & 2 Samuel 1:18

Specifically, the book traces the lineage of Shem, highlighting the generational journey that leads from Shem to Heber, capturing the transitions of time, culture, and events.

It was during the era of Peleg[2], the son of Heber, that a transformative event took place. The world saw a substantial division, not just geographically but culturally and linguistically. This division was not merely a separation of lands but a divergence of ideologies, beliefs, and languages, causing a ripple effect through the generations that followed. (Noha, 1840)

However, to gain a holistic perspective on these events, one cannot solely rely on primary one or two source. While both the Bible and the Book of Jasher mention these pivotal moments, they often summarize. This inherent brevity in their storytelling acts as a call to action for scholars, historians, and curious readers. They are encouraged to venture into supplementary ancient texts, scrolls, and manuscripts, seeking to weave together a more comprehensive and enriched understanding of these foundational tales. By doing so, they hope to unveil layers of context, subtleties, and nuances that might otherwise remain obscured in the annals of history.

The Detailed Account from the Book"of J'bilees:

The Bible and the Book of Jasher provide mere snapshots of a significant event, while the Book of Jubilees offers an intricately detailed tableau. Delving deeper into the narrative, during the onset of the thirty-third jubilee, the Book of Jubilees transports readers to a pivotal historical moment: when Noah and his sons took on the colossal task of dividing the Earth.

---

2   Word means earthquake; during his time Men were divided, and the Earth was divided.

This division wasn't just a mere partition of territories; it set the foundation for the destinies of many tribes and nations that would emerge in the subsequent generations. It laid down the boundaries, not only of land but also of culture, language, and traditions, which would become the bedrock of civilizations.

In the Book of Jubilees, Chapter 8, verses 10 and 11, this monumental occasion is narrated with an eloquence that breathes life into history: "And as the thirty-third jubilee dawned, the Earth was divided into three portions, each to be inherited by Shem, Ham, and Japheth. The profound moment was marked by a ceremony where Noah beckoned his sons and their families. The division was decided by lots, with each son reaching out and drawing a piece of writing from their father, Noah's bosom, revealing their destined portion." (Johnson, 1917)

This portrayal, rich in its detail, invites readers to visualize the gravity and significance of that moment – when decisions made would shape the trajectory of human history for eons to come.

CHAPTER 3

꙳

HOW WAS THE EARTH DIVIDED
HAM'S INHERITANCE

The Land of Africa

For Ham, the second allotment emerged, spanning beyond the Gihon[3] and leaning to the southward flank of the Garden. This vast expanse journeys south, touching the fiery mountains, and winds westward to the Sea of 'Atêl. Stretching further west, it meets the Sea of Mä'ûk— the profound waters that embrace all that remains undestroyed. It ventures northward, brushing the boundaries of Gadìr, then traces the coast, touching the waters until it aligns with the vast sea. Pursuing its course, it comes close to the river Gihon and shadows its banks, ultimately uniting with the eastern confines of the Garden of Eden. Thus, this vast land is the inheritance bestowed upon Ham, an eternal dwelling for him and his lineage, destined to remain for himself and his sons unto their generations forever.

---

3   Genesis 2:13 It is often associated with regions such as Cush sometimes identified with parts of modern-day Ethiopia

Geographical Markers of Ham's Territory:	
Direction	Landmark/Description
South	Beyond the Gihon, towards the Garden
South	Touches the fiery mountains
West	To the Sea of 'Atêl
West	Meets the Sea of Mä'ûk
North	Brushes boundaries of Gadìr
North-West	Aligns with the vast sea
North-East	Close to river Gihon
East	Garden of Eden

Japheth's Inheritance: The Expanses of North Asia, Europe, and the Five Prominent Isles

The third allocation, designated for Japheth, spanned northward beyond the river Tina[4]. This tract unfurled northeast, encompassing the vast lands of Gog and all territories to its east. Journeying further north, it touched the towering mountains of Qêlt, heading towards the Sea of Mä'ûk and meandering eastward, skirting the edges of Gâdir, reaching the vast waters of the sea. From there, it curved westward, nearing Färd, before arching back towards 'Afêrâg. Stretching east, it embraced the waters of the Sea of Mê'at. Proceeding, it traced the river Tînâ's path northeast until the river's boundary, where it spiraled back northward around the majestic mountain Rafa. (Johnson, 1917)

Such is the vast expanse destined for Japheth and his lineage—an inheritance comprising five grand isles and an expansive northern territory. This land, characterized by its cold temperament, contrasts with Ham's warm realm and Shem's temperate lands, a blend of cool and warm.

---

4   Likely corresponds to the Oxis River, which is now known as the Amu Darya in Central Asia.

Geographical Markers of Japheth's Territory:	
Rivers and Waters:	
Tina River	Oxis River (Amu Darya)
Tanis River	Don River (Russia)
Me'at Sea	(Sea of Azov)
Gihon River	Ganges
Ma'uk Sea	(Baltic Sea)
Egyptian Sea	(Red Sea)
Great Sea	(Mediterranean Sea)
Mountains and Ranges:	
Rafa Mountains	Himalayan & Pamir Mountian
Tarus Mountains	Southern Turkey Euphrates flow from Tarus
Amanus Mountains	Nur Mountain in S Turkey
Libabus Mountains	Lebanon
Celtic Mountains	Pyrenees
Key Cities and Regions:	
Karaso	Cadiz/Gadir (Cadiz, Spain)
Fara	Africa
"Aferag"	Africa
Noteworthy Islands:	
Balearic	Sicily
Sardinia	Corsica
Cyprus	
This territorial expanse encapsulates the grandeur and vastness that Japheth and his descendants would come to know as home, a land distinguished by its unique geography and climatic variations.* (Johnson, 1917)	

Shem's Inheritance

"Blessed be the Lord God of Shem, and may the Lord dwell in the dwelling of Shem"

The Sacred Inheritance of Shem:
Middle East, India, and China

In the division of the post-Flood world, Shem's portion emerged as an extraordinary responsibility, encompassing regions of profound historical and spiritual significance, including the Middle East, India, and China. Noah's blessing, "Blessed be the Lord God of Shem, And may the Lord dwell in the dwelling of Shem,"[5] underscores the sacred nature of this inheritance. Let us explore the profound responsibilities and the importance of Shem's land.

The Middle East: The Cradle of Civilization

Shem's portion, comprising the Middle East, holds a unique place in human history. It is in this region that early civilizations such as Mesopotamia, Egypt, and the Levant flourished. The birth of monotheistic faiths, including Judaism, Christianity, and Islam, occurred here. The divine blessing bestowed upon Shem recognizes the Middle East as a spiritual epicenter, where the oneness of God was proclaimed, shaping the course of religious thought for millennia.

India: A Rich Heritage of Spirituality

Shem's portion extends into the Indian subcontinent, a land known for its rich spiritual traditions. From Hinduism to Buddhism,

---

5   Genesis 9:26

Jainism to Sikhism, India has been a wellspring of profound philosophical and religious thought. The divine command that allocated this land to Shem underscores the importance of preserving and nurturing these spiritual traditions, promoting tolerance and the search for divine truth.

China: Ancient Wisdom and Civilization

China, part of Shem's portion, boasts one of the world's oldest civilizations. Its philosophical traditions, including Confucianism and Taoism, have profoundly influenced human thought. The responsibility to steward this land acknowledges its contributions to ethics, governance, and the pursuit of harmony. Shem's descendants are entrusted with the duty to safeguard and share the wisdom that has emerged from China's ancient culture.

Noah's Rejoice and Prophecy

Noah's joy upon Shem's portion coming forth is a testament to the significance of this inheritance. His prophecy, **"Blessed be the Lord God of Shem, And may the Lord dwell in the dwelling of Shem,"** reinforces the sacred nature of Shem's responsibility. It is a recognition that in these lands, the divine presence can be felt, and a profound covenant exists between God and Shem's descendants.

Shem's primary responsibility is to preserve the belief in one God and the moral guidance inherent in monotheistic faiths. The Middle East, India, and China have historically been beacons of spiritual enlightenment. Shem's descendants are entrusted with maintaining this light and ensuring that it continues illuminating the path of righteousness for humanity.

Noah's Blessing as a Continuing Legacy

Noah's blessing upon Shem's portion echoes through the corridors of time. It serves as a reminder that these lands are not merely geographical territories but sacred trusts. They are places where the divine and the human intersect, where seekers of truth and faith find common ground. Noah's rejoicing and prophecy stand as a testament to the enduring spiritual legacy that continues to shape these regions today.

Exploring Shem's inheritance invites a deeper reflection on the immense significance of this hallowed legacy and its lasting influence on both human spirituality and the evolution of civilizations. The vast territories encompassing the Middle East, India, and China symbolize divine intervention. They are treasure troves of age-old wisdom, bequeathed to successive generations to elevate the human spirit. In the detailed annals penned by Josephus, specifically in Chapter 6, verse 4, the territorial dominion of Shem is corroborated. As the third son of Noah, Shem had five sons who inhabited the vast expanse from the Euphrates to the distant shores of the Indian Ocean[6].

---

6   Josephus 6:4

Geographical Markers of Shem's Territory:	
Feature/Region	Description
Central Location	Middle of the earth
Starting Point	Middle of the mountain range of Rafa to the mouth of the water from the river Tina
Western Boundary	Extends till the water of the abysses. Goes towards the great sea named the tongue of the Egyptian Sea
Southern Boundary	Extends till it reaches the west of the tongue, looking towards the south. Goes to 'Afra and the waters of the river Gihon
Eastern Boundary	Extends till it reaches the Garden of Eden to its south. Continues till it reaches the east of the mountain named Rafa and descends to the mouth of the river Tina
Noteworthy Territories	Garden of Eden (holy of holies and dwelling of the Lord), Mount Sinai (center of the desert), Mount Zion (center of the navel of the earth)
Associated Blessings	Land of Eden, Red Sea, east land, India, Red Sea's mountains, Bashan, Lebanon, Kaftur islands, Sanir mountains, 'Amana mountains, Asshur mountains
Further Territories	Elam, Asshur, Babel, Susan, Ma'edai, Ararat mountains, a region beyond the sea which is beyond the mountains of Asshur

The Dead Sea Scrolls

Importantly, the Dead Sea Scrolls, especially in the 'Tales of the Patriarchs' section, known as '1QAPGEN,' intricately describe the distribution of lands among Noah's sons: Shem, Ham, and Japheth. This text sheds light on the historical context of this division. According to Column 17, 'Shem divided his inheritance among his sons. To Elam, the eldest, he assigned the northern territories along the Tigris River, extending to the Red Sea and up north to the river's source. The boundary then shifted westward towards Ashur's land, reaching the point of convergence with the Tigris.' (The Dead Sea Scrolls, 2005) The passage continues with further details on the lands apportioned to the other brothers."

CHAPTER 4

⌘

THE LAND OF MANY NAMES.

Having broken down the distribution of territories among Noah's descendants, our attention now shifts to a region of paramount significance: **the land of Canaan.** This iconic land, with its layers of history, cultural intersections, and strategic importance, has often been at the heart of countless narratives, both sacred and secular. Through different periods, as empires rose and fell and as various civilizations made their mark, this land witnessed a multitude of name changes that reflected its evolving geopolitical and cultural landscape.

The land of Canaan, a focal point in many ancient writings, has seen empires clash and cultures blend. It has been a cradle for religious events and a melting pot of ancient civilizations. Beyond its strategic location, it stands as a testament to human history's complexity, hosting a multitude of peoples and ideologies over the ages.

As we journey deeper into its intricate history, it's essential to recognize the diverse titles this land has been known by, each name offering a unique window into a specific era or significant event. These varied designations provide insight into the socio-political dynamics of the time but also illuminate the cultural, religious, and historical contexts that shaped the region. Let's delve into a comprehensive exploration of these names, tracing back the legacy of a land that has continually captured the imagination of generations.

Canaan: This is the earliest known name for the region, as mentioned in ancient Egyptian records and the Hebrew Bible. The Canaanites were the original inhabitants of the land.[7]

Promised Land: This term originates from the Bible, referring to the territory God promised to the descendants of Abraham, specifically to the lineage of Isaac and Jacob (the Israelites). (Bright, 2000)

Land of Israel: After the Exodus from Egypt, the Israelites conquered parts of Canaan and established the Kingdoms of Israel and Judah. The land thus became known as the Land of Israel. (Finkelstein, The Bible Unearthed: Archaeology's New Vision of Ancient Israel and the Origin of Its Sacred Texts. (2001))

Judah or Judea: After the split of the Kingdom of Israel, the southern part became known as the Kingdom of Judah. Later, under Roman rule, it was named the Province of Judea. (Finkelstein, (2001))

Palestine: This name is derived from "Philistia," referencing the Philistines, an Aegean people who settled on the southern coast of the land during the early Iron Age. Over time, the Romans and subsequent empires used "Palestina" or "Palaestina" to refer to the broader region. (Tubb, 1998))

---

7   The Holy Bible. Genesis 10:15-19.

      Petrie, W.M.F. (1891). *Egypt and Israel*. London: Nutt. (This book elaborates on the Egyptian records mentioning Canaan and its association with the Canaanites.)

Holy Land: Given its religious significance to Judaism, Christianity, and Islam, the region has often been referred to as the "Holy Land." (Armstrong, 1997)

Bilad al-Sham: During the Islamic Caliphates, especially the Umayyad and Abbasid periods, the region was part of a larger province known as Bilad al-Sham, or simply "al-Sham," which covered greater Syria and surrounding areas. (Kennedy, 2004)

Mandatory Palestine: After World War I, the land came under British control as the "British Mandate for Palestine." (Khalidi, 2006)

State of Israel: In 1948, following the end of the British Mandate, the State of Israel was established on part of this land. (Morris, 2008)

West Bank: After the 1948 Arab-Israeli War, the Jordan River's western bank area was annexed by Jordan and became commonly known as the West Bank. After 1967, it came under Israeli control. (Gelvin, 2005)

The land, which was historically referred to as Canaan and is presently known as Israel, holds profound significance in the annals of history. Entrusted to Shem and his lineage, this stretch of territory wasn't just a piece of land but a symbol of legacy and heritage. The solemn oath taken, a covenant binding in nature, ensured that Shem and every generation that followed would be the **rightful custodians** of this sacred ground. Throughout time, this decree has stood as a testament to the enduring connection between the descendants of Shem and the land of Canaan, emphasizing that their bond isn't merely transient or of the moment but **eternal**. The rich tapestry of stories, traditions, and cultures that have since evolved is deeply rooted in this land, making it not just a physical space but a spiritual home meant to be held, honored, and passed down through the corridors of time.

THE GENEALOGY OF JAPHETH

According to the Hebrew Bible, particularly in the book of Genesis, Japheth was one of the three sons of Noah. After the flood, the descendants of Japheth's sons are said to have settled in various regions, and they are often associated with Indo-European populations.

The descendants of Japheth, as listed in Genesis 10, include:

Gomer: His descendants are believed to be the ancestors of early groups in Anatolia (modern-day Turkey). The sons of Gomer mentioned are:

Ashkenaz: Possibly associated with the Scythians and, later on, the name was related to the Ashkenazi Jews.

Riphath: Exact identification is uncertain.

Togarmah: Might be associated with the Armenians or other Anatolian groups.

Magog: The identity of Magog's descendants is debated, but they are sometimes associated with the Scythians or other northern tribes.

Madai: Often identified with the Medes, who lived in what is now western Iran.

Javan: Traditionally associated with the Ionians or the Greeks. The sons of Javan include:

Elishah: Possibly associated with the Aegean region or Cyprus.

Tarshish: Its location is debated, but it could be related to southern Spain (Tartessos) or Tarsus in Anatolia.

Kittim: Generally identified with Cyprus.

Dodanim (or Rodanim): Possibly linked to the island of Rhodes or other locations in the eastern Mediterranean.

Tubal: Often identified with ancient tribes in eastern Anatolia, near the Black Sea.

Meshech: Associated with tribes in Anatolia, possibly near modern-day Moscow or the Black Sea region.

Tiras: The exact identity of Tiras's descendants is uncertain, but they may be related to the Thracians or other groups in the Aegean or Black Sea region.

The identities and locations associated with many of these names are based on a combination of biblical, historical, and linguistic sources, and there's often debate among scholars about precise identifications. However, in the biblical narrative, the descendants of Japheth are generally thought to have settled in the northern and western parts of the known world, covering parts of Europe and western Asia.

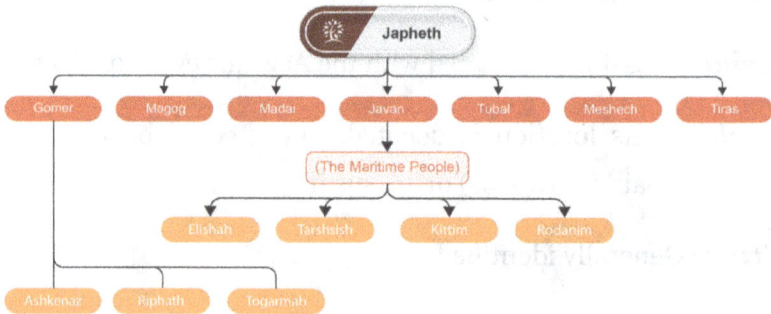

The Genealogy of Japheth

THE GENEALOGY OF HAM

Ham, one of Noah's three sons, had several descendants, according to biblical records. Here's a list of Ham's immediate descendants, often referred to as the nations or tribes associated with them:

Cush (often associated with ancient Nubia or modern-day Sudan)

Location: Cush is typically equated with ancient Nubia, situated south of Egypt, aligning with present-day Sudan. Influential kingdoms mark the realm of the Cushites.

Significance: Among the notable Cushites is Nimrod, biblically depicted as a formidable king and hunter. He's credited with the foundation of pivotal cities such as Babel (likely Babylon), Erech (Uruk), and Akkad in Shinar's region, which may hint at ancient Mesopotamia or Sumer.

Mizraim (commonly identified with Egypt)

Location: Mizraim translates to Egypt in Hebrew; hence, his descendants correspond to various ancient Egyptian dynasties and factions.

Significance: Egypt holds an iconic stance in biblical lore. It's not only the setting for Joseph's saga but also the birthplace of Moses' mission to free the Israelites. The legacy of the Pharaohs, the iconic pyramids, and the Nile's rich civilization find their lineage in Mizraim.

Phut (commonly linked with regions in North Africa, particularly Libya)

Location: Phut is often connected to regions in North Africa, with a strong association with today's Libya.

Significance: Phut's descendants were presumably recognized for their martial prowess, given their mentions alongside combat scenarios in scriptures like Ezekiel and Jeremiah.

Canaan (progenitor of the Canaanites)

Descendants: Key descendants include Sidon (his eldest), Heth, the Jebusites, the Amorites, the Girgashites, the Hivites, the Arkites, the Sinites, the Arvadites, the Zemarites, and the Hamathites.

Location: Geographically, Canaan covers today's Israel, Palestine, Lebanon, and parts of Syria and Jordan.

Significance: Canaan and his lineage hold paramount importance in biblical tales. The Canaanites settled in the land that would later be divinely promised to Abraham's lineage, becoming central to numerous biblical episodes. For instance:

Sidon: Renowned as an ancient maritime and trading hub.

Heth: Precursors to the Hittites, a formidable power of the ancient Near East.

Tribes such as the Jebusites, Amorites, and Girgashites: Often referenced during Israel's acquisition of the promised land, residing in various regions that were to become Israelite domains.

The Genealogy of Ham

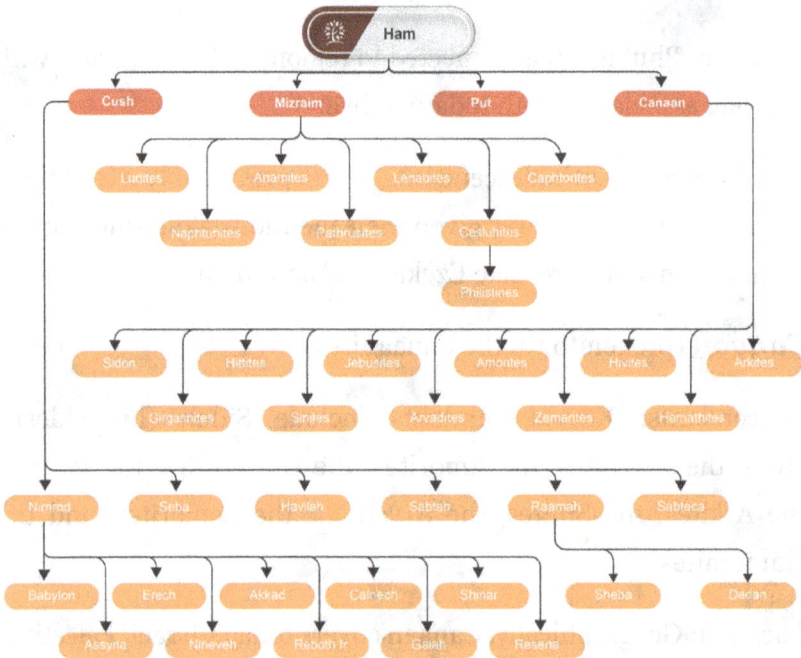

In biblical tradition, these names embody the initial tribes or nations birthed from Ham. Among them, particularly the Canaanites, are integral to biblical tales, given that Canaan represents the territory divinely bequeathed to Abraham and his progeny.

THE GENEALOGY FROM SHEM TO ABRAHAM

Delving into the annals of biblical history, one encounters a lineage that forms the bedrock of many modern faiths: the genealogy from Shem to Abraham. This lineage, preserved in the Book of Genesis, is a testament to the divine narrative and the foreordained destiny of a chosen people.

Shem: As a direct descendant of Noah, Shem stands prominently as one of his three sons. Within tradition, he is viewed as the progenitor of the Semitic races. His role in this lineage is paramount as the foundational figure leading to Abraham.

Arpachshad, a cornerstone in the lineage of Shem, played an essential role as a conduit between Shem's era and the subsequent dynasties. Renowned as the progenitors of the Chaldeans[8], their domain witnessed the rise of the city of Ur — the birthplace of Abram, who would later be known as Abraham and in this vast expanse designated to Shem, esteemed patriarchs such as Nahor, Abraham's grandfather, and Terah, his father, also staked their roots, further solidifying the significance of Shem's territories in the annals of history.

Shelah: The lineage advances with Arpachshad's offspring, Shelah, further weaving the intricate tapestry leading to Abraham.

Heber: From Shelah came forth Heber. Historically significant, the name "Hebrew" is conjectured to have its roots from Heber,[9] tying him intrinsically to the identity of the Israelites.

---

8   From the Complete works of Josephus

9   From the Complete works of Josephus Chapter 6 vs 4

Peleg: Following Heber, Peleg emerges in this ancestral line. His very name, signifying "division," reflects the epochal event of his time — the earth's division and the division of people, which some interpret as the dispersion at the Tower of Babel.

Reu: The lineage continues to flourish with Reu, the offspring of Peleg, marking another step in this divine genealogical journey.

Serug: From Reu comes Serug, further solidifying the familial ties that bind these generations together.

Nahor: Serug begets Nahor, another integral link in this chain leading to the birth of a nation.

Terah: Nahor's lineage produces Terah, bringing us closer to a figure pivotal to the narrative of monotheistic religions.

Abraham (Initially known as Abram): Terah's legacy is most prominently marked by his son Abram, later known as Abraham. As the progenitor of the Israelites, Abraham's covenant with God positions him as a central figure in Jewish, Christian, and Islamic traditions.

This lineage, stretching from Shem to Abraham, showcases a divine narrative intricately woven through generations. It underscores the unwavering faith and destiny of a people chosen to bear the torch of monotheism. Through these names and their stories, we gain insight into the foundation and propagation of a faith that has shaped civilizations for millennia.

Shem - One of Noah's three sons.
Arpachshad - Son of Shem.
Shelah - Son of Arpachshad.

Heber - Son of Shelah. Notably, the term "Hebrew" may be derived from his name.

Peleg - Son of Eber.

Reu - Son of Peleg.

Serug - Son of Reu.

Nahor - Son of Serug.

Terah - Son of Nahor.

Abraham - One of the three sons of Terah. The others are Nahor and Haran. Abraham was the tenth from Noah and was born in the two hundred and ninety-second year after the flood.[10]

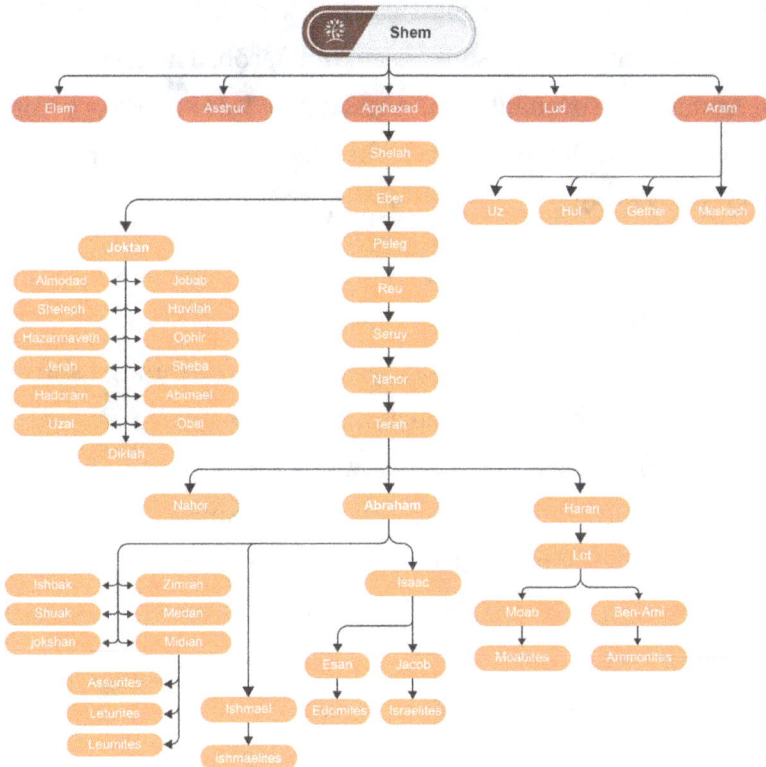

The Genealogy of Shem

---

10   Flavius Josephus; The Complete works Chapter 6v5

THE GENEALOGY FROM ABRAHAM TO ISRAEL

Abraham, originally known as Abram, is a central and revered figure across the world's major monotheistic religions, including Judaism, Christianity, and Islam. His journey in the bible begins with a divine call from God to leave his homeland and embark on a voyage to Canaan, where God pledges to bless him with descendants who will become a great nation. A significant part of Abraham's story revolves around overcoming the challenge of infertility with his wife Sarah, ultimately witnessing the miraculous birth of their son Isaac in their old age.

Isaac, the heir of Abraham and Sarah, takes up the mantle of the family's lineage. He marries Rebekah, and together, they become parents to twin sons, Esau and Jacob. The transition of the Abrahamic covenant from Abraham to Isaac marks a pivotal moment within this lineage, solidifying the divine promises for generations to come.

Jacob, originally named "heel-grabber" or "supplanter," plays a multifaceted role in biblical history. His most notable feat involves securing Esau's birthright and blessing through shrewd means. Yet, Jacob's journey takes a transformative turn when he wrestles with a divine being, leading to a name change—Israel—a name that carries profound spiritual significance. Jacob's life is further marked by his twelve sons, born to his two wives, Leah and Rachel, and their maids, Bilhah and Zilpah. Each of these sons becomes the patriarch of one of the twelve tribes of Israel, forming the bedrock of the nation of Israel.

These twelve tribes, each with its distinct territory, responsibilities, and place within the community, collectively represent the nation of Israel. Notable among these tribes are Ephraim and Manasseh, often associated with the northern kingdom of Israel following the division of the nation.

At the heart of this lineage lies the Abrahamic covenant—a divine pact initiated with Abraham, continued through Isaac and Jacob. This covenant encompasses promises of land, countless descendants, and divine blessings. It stands as a foundational narrative within the Bible, significantly influencing the identity, history, and faith of the Jewish people. As the Israelites traverse from Egypt to the land of Canaan, the covenant's promises unfold, epitomizing the transformative power of faith and perseverance.

The genealogy from Abraham to Israel **(Jacob)** can be traced through the biblical accounts found primarily in the Book of Genesis. Here is the lineage:

1. **Abraham** (Originally Abram): Abraham is the father of the Jewish, Christian, and Islamic faiths. He married Sarah and had several children, but the most significant lineage comes through his son Isaac.

2. **Isaac:** Isaac was the son of Abraham and Sarah. He married Rebekah, and they had two sons, Esau and Jacob. The promised lineage continues through Jacob.

3. **Jacob** (Originally named Jacob, later renamed Israel): Jacob, whose name was changed to Israel by God, had twelve sons. These twelve sons became the patriarchs of

the twelve tribes of Israel, which are the foundation of the nation of Israel. Here are the names of Jacob's twelve sons:

a. Reuben
b. Simeon
c. Levi
d. Judah
e. Dan
f. Naphtali
g. Gad
h. Asher
i. Issachar
j. Zebulun
k. Joseph
l. Benjamin

13. The Twelve Tribes of Israel: Each of Jacob's sons became the father of one of the twelve tribes of Israel. These tribes are foundational to the history, identity, and organization of the people of Israel.

CHAPTER 5

∾᪳᪲᪰

"And they all said, 'So be it; so be it.'"

LINKING THE DOTS.

Shem's story starts long ago and holds a special place in ancient scriptures. His family, over time, became deeply tied to the region known as Canaan. The descendants of Shem weren't just passive observers; they actively shaped the region's history, culture, and identity.

From great leaders to common folk, the members of Shem's lineage played various roles, both big and small, in the unfolding saga of Canaan. As pioneers, they established cities and trade routes; as leaders, they provided guidance; and as residents, they infused the land with their customs, beliefs, and traditions.

Beyond the walls of cities and towns, the natural landscapes of Canaan also bore witness to their journeys, struggles, and celebrations. The mountains, rivers, and valleys became integral to their stories, often as backdrops for significant events and milestones.

As generations passed, stories of Shem's family were told and retold, intertwining their legacy with the tales of Canaan. New generations built upon the foundations set by their ancestors, ensuring that the bond between Shem's descendants and the land remained unbroken.

In sum, Shem's family, through countless generations, wove a narrative that is inseparable from the land of Canaan, making their bond a vital chapter in the grand story of the region. Let's embark on a journey to unravel the intricate tapestry of Shem's lineage and explore their timeless connection to the land once called Canaan.

THE SACRED BLESSING

Following this division, Noah, in a momentous act, bound his sons by an oath and cursed any attempts to seize unallotted portions.

After the division of the Earth among his three sons—Shem, Ham, and Japheth—Noah proceeded to bestow a blessing upon them. This blessing was not a mere formality but carried significant weight and implications for future generations, its impact still resonates in today's world. Noah, as the patriarch of his family and the one chosen by God to survive the great flood, held a unique authority. In this context, his blessing had several key aspects:

Spiritual Authority: As a righteous man who had found favor in the eyes of the Lord, Noah's blessing was seen as spiritually authoritative. It carried divine significance and was believed to shape the destinies of his sons and their descendants.

Stewardship of the Earth: Through the division of the land, Noah entrusted each of his sons with specific territories. This act of division was more than just a practical arrangement; it symbolized the stewardship of the Earth's resources. Each son was responsible for cultivating and maintaining the land allotted to him.

Oath and Covenant: Noah bound his sons by an oath during this blessing. By doing so, he invoked a sacred covenant—a solemn agreement with divine consequences. This oath underscored the seriousness of the division and the consequences of violating it.

Curses and Blessings: Noah's blessing was not without its conditions. He pronounced curses on anyone who sought to seize a portion of land not allotted to them by the divine lot. This served as a stern warning against disputes and land encroachments among his descendants.

Prophetic Element: Noah's blessing also had a prophetic dimension. He had insights into the futures of his sons and the nations that would descend from them. These prophecies would guide the understanding of future generations regarding their roles and destinies.

In essence, Noah's blessing was a momentous event that set the course for the post-flood world. It established a framework for the relationship between his sons, their territories, and the spiritual and moral responsibilities associated with their stewardship. The curses and blessings attached to this division underscored the gravity of adhering to divine decrees and maintaining the harmony of the newly reborn world. Through these blessings, Noah left a lasting legacy that continues to influence the course of human history.

OATH AND COVENANT

In a solemn and momentous ceremony, the sons of Noah undertook the division of the Earth among their own sons, all of which took place in the presence of their father, Noah. As the patriarch of their lineage, Noah held a unique and spiritually significant role during this division.

In this sacred moment, Noah did not merely observe; he played a central role by binding all of his sons with a solemn oath. This oath was no ordinary pledge but a binding agreement invoked divine consequences. It included a severe curse upon anyone who dared to overstep their allotted portion of land, determined through the casting of lots.

And thus the sons of Noah divided unto their sons in the presence of Noah, their father, and he bound them all by an oath, imprecating a **curse** on everyone that sought to seize the portion which had not fallen (to him) by his lot.

And they all said, **'So be it; so be it** '[11] for themselves and their sons forever **throughout their generations till the day of judgment**, on which the Lord God shall judge them with a sword and with fire for all the unclean wickedness of their errors, wherewith they have filled the earth with transgression and uncleanness and fornication and sin. (Johnson, 1917)

Remarkably, Noah's sons and their descendants willingly accepted this oath with the resounding declaration, "So be it; so be it." This acceptance signified their commitment to honor the conditions set forth, highlighting the gravity of the oath. Importantly, this

---

11   *Jubliees Chapter 9:15*

binding oath was intended to extend throughout generations, safeguarding the sanctity of the land division.

Noah, possessing a unique understanding of the divine order and the consequences of human actions, foresaw a day of reckoning in the future. This day of judgment was envisioned as an event when the Lord God would execute justice with a sword and fire, signifying divine retribution for the unclean wickedness, errors, transgressions, uncleanness, fornication, and sin that had plagued the Earth.

In essence, Noah's Blessing was not just a division of land; it was a sacred covenant, with the curse serving as a powerful deterrent against land disputes and wrongful seizures. This blessing and oath were deeply rooted in Noah's profound wisdom and his unwavering belief in the need for humanity to adhere to divine principles to establish a just and righteous world. This sacred moment held both spiritual significance and practical implications, laying the foundation for the post-flood world and shaping the destinies of generations to come.

The consequences of the oath that Noah bound his sons and their descendants by were profound and far-reaching. This solemn commitment carried significant weight and implications for generations to come:

Divine Consequences: At its core, this oath invoked divine consequences. It was not merely a human agreement but a sacred covenant sealed with spiritual authority. Those who violated it would face repercussions that extended beyond earthly matters.

Curse for Unlawful Seizures: Central to the oath was a curse pronounced on anyone who sought to seize a portion of land not allotted to them by the divine casting of lots. This curse was a powerful deterrent against land disputes and wrongful land seizures.

Preservation of Divine Order: The oath served to preserve the divine order as envisioned by Noah. It was a mechanism to maintain the sanctity of the land division and ensure that each son and their descendants adhered to their allotted territories.

Generational Commitment: Importantly, the oath was not limited to the immediate generation but was intended to extend throughout generations. It signified an enduring commitment to divine principles and the sanctity of land distribution.

Day of Judgment: Noah, with his deep spiritual insight, foresaw a day of judgment in the future. This day was seen as a divine reckoning, where the Lord God would execute justice with a sword and fire. The oath was a reminder that actions in the present would have consequences in the future.

Spiritual Significance: The oath held profound spiritual significance. It reinforced the belief that human actions were not separate from divine judgment and that adherence to divine principles was paramount in maintaining righteousness.

Foundation for a Just World: Ultimately, the oath and its consequences laid the foundation for a just and orderly world. It was a recognition that adhering to divine principles, respecting boundaries, and avoiding wrongful actions were essential for the harmonious coexistence of humanity.

VIOLATION OF THE OATH

In the context of the passage, Canaan emerges as a significant biblical figure among the descendants of Noah, being one of the sons of Ham, who, along with Shem and Japheth, constitutes the trio of Noah's sons. This narrative is documented in the Book of Jubilees, an ancient Jewish text that provides additional insights into events and characters mentioned in the Bible.

The crux of Canaan's significance within this narrative centers on his actions regarding the division of land among Noah's sons. According to the text, Canaan made the fateful decision to settle in a territory that had not been allocated to him in the divine division orchestrated by Noah. While this decision might seem inconsequential at first glance, its consequences were profound, ultimately leading to disputes and discord within his own family, repercussions that have persisted for generations, even to this very day.

In the Book of Jubilees, Chapter 10, Verse 28, Canaan purposefully goes against his father's agreement. The text explains, "And Ham and his sons went into the land which he was to occupy, which he acquired as his portion in the land of the south." Despite this, Canaan, enticed by the rich and fertile Lebanese territory that stretched from the river of Egypt to the sea, decided to settle there. This act of settling in Lebanon, covering areas to the east and west of the Jordan River and the sea, was a direct violation of the established division of land among Noah's descendants.

Canaan's actions and the subsequent repercussions serve as a poignant example, underscoring the paramount importance of adhering to divine decrees and the gravity associated with disrupting the established order. The blessings imparted by Noah carried significant weight, and the curses invoked for those who wrongfully seized land underscored the sanctity of the divine plan.

Canaan's audacious choice to settle in unassigned territory not only challenged the divine order established by Noah but also set the stage for a legacy marked by territorial disputes, conflicts, and the enduring struggles of diverse nations for control over this historically significant land to this day.

In the narrative from Jubilees, Canaan's decision to settle in an unallocated land is met with strong opposition from his family, including his father Ham and brothers, Cush and Mizraim. They understood the severity of his actions and tried to dissuade him, highlighting the dire consequences of inhabiting a land not destined for them. This wasn't just a family disagreement but a breach of the sacred covenant established through Noah. They warned Canaan that such actions could lead to curses and strife among their descendants. Jubilees 10:30 captures their admonition, **"And Ham, his father, and Cush and Mizraim, his brothers, said unto him: 'Thou hast settled in a land which is not thine, and which did not fall to us by lot: do not do so; for if thou dost do so, thou and thy sons will fall in the land and (be) accursed through sedition; for by sedition ye have settled, and by sedition will thy children fall, and thou shalt be rooted out forever.'"**

Jubilees further elaborates on how Canaan receives a stern warning for his significant breach of the family's sacred agreements. Verse 31 states, **'Dwell not in the dwelling of Shem; for to Shem**

and his sons did it come by their lot.' Following this, he is harshly cursed: 'Cursed art thou, and cursed shalt thou be beyond all the sons of Noah, by the curse by which we bound ourselves by an oath in the presence of the holy judge, and in the presence of Noah our father.

"Despite the solemn warnings and the potential for dire consequences, Canaan remained steadfast in occupying the land. His unwavering determination to keep his claim on this territory has left a lasting impact on history, reshaping the destiny of nations. As a result, this region became known as Canaan, as stated in verse 34: **'And for this reason, that land is named Canaan.'** This name has become forever associated with a legacy of territorial disputes, conflicts, and ongoing struggles among various nations for control over this historically significant land. Canaan's actions, marked by defiance of divine order, serve as an enduring lesson about the repercussions of challenging the divine plan - a decision whose effects continue to resonate today.

CHAPTER 6

∽⊶∾

'To your descendants, I give this land, from the Wadi of
Egypt to the great river, the Euphrates. **Gen 15:18**

ABRAHAM'S PROMISE

The consensus among historians and biblical scholars is that
the land known as Canaan, later renamed Israel, was divinely
promised to Abraham, as stated in Genesis 15:18. This widespread
belief positions Abraham as the starting point of God's covenant
concerning the land. However, a deeper exploration into extra-
biblical texts reveals that this spiritual and historical connection
to the land predates Abraham, tracing back to Shem, Noah's
son. The lineage from Shem to Abraham spans ten generations,
including Arphaxad, Shelah, Eber, Peleg, Reu, Serug, Nahor,
and Terah. Detailed in the Book of Jubilees, this ten-generation
lineage indicates that the land rights were established well before
Abraham, underscoring a more ancient and profound bond
between Abraham's ancestors and the promised land.

The Promise of Land:
In the passage of Genesis 12:1-3, God commands Abram to
leave his homeland and family for a land yet to be revealed.
This profound directive comes with a promise of monumental
blessings: transforming Abram into a great nation, bestowing

upon him immense blessings and a revered name, and making him a conduit of blessings for all people on earth. "I will bless those who bless you, and whoever curses you I will curse." This promise not only underscores a physical relocation but also signifies the unfolding of a significant divine plan. As Abraham embarks on this journey, the specifics of this promised land gradually unfold, marking a pivotal moment in biblical history.

In Genesis 15:18-21, a more expansive depiction of the promised land is given:
"On that day, the LORD made a covenant with Abram, saying, 'To your descendants, I give this land, from the Wadi of Egypt to the great river, the Euphrates— the land of the Kenites, Kenizzites, Kadmonites, Hittites, Perizzites, Rephaites, Amorites, Canaanites, Girgashites, and Jebusites.'" Intriguingly, these tribes are descendants of Ham.

This description outlines a vast area in the Middle East, rich in history and diversity. The covenant encompasses lands inhabited by various groups, each with their unique cultures and histories, indicating the breadth and significance of the territory promised to Abraham's descendants. This vast region, promised to Abraham, would become a central aspect of the biblical narrative, shaping the course of history for these tribes and the emerging nation of Israel.

The Significance of Shem:

As previously mentioned, Abraham was a descendant of Shem, one of the three sons of Noah. The Genesis 10 'Table of Nations' shows that Shem's lineage inherited and settled in lands in the Middle East, **the same region promised to Abraham.**

The post-flood land distribution among Noah's sons, Shem, Ham, and Japheth, holds significant meaning in the biblical context. Each son received a distinct portion of the earth as their inheritance. This division was more than a geographical allocation; it encompassed spiritual and covenantal aspects, reflecting deeper dimensions of the biblical story.

God's Respect for Boundaries:

God's promise to Abraham about the land is a significant and defining moment in biblical history. This promise wasn't just about territory; it was intricately connected to God's broader plan for humanity and His relationship with a chosen people.

When observing the delineation of territories among Noah's sons, it's fascinating to note that Abraham's inheritance was situated within the boarders of **Shem's territory**. This wasn't an arbitrary decision. It was a conscious act that revealed God's respect for the divisions and arrangements made after the deluge. Even though God possesses the power to reshape and redefine, He chose to work within the boundaries previously set, emphasizing His commitment to human choices and established agreements.

Diving deeper into the importance of territories, it's evident that land was more than just physical space in biblical times. It carried a spiritual, cultural, and familial significance. Land was an extension of one's identity, lineage, and covenant with the Divine. The territories assigned to Shem, Ham, and Japheth were not mere geographical divisions but symbolized their unique roles and destinies in the unfolding of human history.

Considering this, the notion that God would steer clear of promising Abraham a portion of land designated for Ham or

Japheth becomes even more profound. It serves as a testament to God's unerring faithfulness to His word. By ensuring Abraham's promise remained within Shem's domain, God reinforced the sanctity of His covenant, the value He places on integrity, and His unwavering respect for established pacts.

Moreover, this promise played a pivotal role in shaping the identity of the Israelites. The land of Canaan wasn't just a piece of real estate; it was the tangible manifestation of God's promise and favor. As descendants of Abraham, the Israelites knew that Canaan[12] was their divinely ordained homeland, and this knowledge profoundly influenced their actions, aspirations, and interactions with neighboring nations.

The precise manner in which God allocated the land to Abraham, ensuring it was within Shem's purview, showcases His meticulous nature and adherence to His word. It is a profound reminder of the weight and value of divine promises. This specific allocation not only influenced the destiny of the Israelites but also echoed the importance of honoring and recognizing the divisions and covenants established among the descendants of Noah.

JOSHUA AND THE CANAANITES

The passage recounting Canaan's actions, wherein he settled in a land not designated for him, delves into the profound implications of disobedience to divine directives and territorial claims. Canaan's bold decision to occupy a portion of land meant for Shem and his descendants, defying the divine lot cast by Noah and the solemn oath taken by Noah and his sons, serves as a stark illustration of

12   For Canaan settling in unallocated territory belonging to Shem and his descendance

the violation of their oath and disobedience against God's intended plan for dividing the land among Noah's descendants.

However, it's essential to recognize that this disobedience wasn't just a matter of territorial boundaries. It carried a more profound significance—it challenged divine authority and order, as established by Noah and, by extension, by God. Canaan's encroachment upon this land without rightful ownership, flouting the divine order, foreshadowed the inevitable consequences of such disobedience, symbolized by the curses pronounced and the notion of being uprooted from the land. **'Cursed art thou, and cursed shalt thou be beyond all the sons of Noah, by the curse by which we bound ourselves by an oath in the presence of the holy judge, and in the presence of Noah our father'.**

Now, let's provide some context by drawing a parallel between the biblical account of Moses leading the children of Israel out of Egypt into the wilderness and the subsequent events led by Joshua in the Book of Joshua:

Moses, Israel's first leader, played a pivotal role in leading the children of Israel out of Egypt and guiding them through the wilderness toward the Promised Land. As previously discussed, the Promised Land was God's designated territory for the descendants of Shem through Abraham, with a particular emphasis on the children of Israel as the rightful heirs.

After the death of Moses, Joshua became the leader of the Israelites. Under Joshua's leadership, the Israelites continued to pursue the divine command from God to embark on a conquest of the land of Canaan. This land was inhabited by various indigenous peoples, most notably the Canaanites. The divine command was, in essence, a fulfillment of the legacy established by Noah's division of land. In that ancient division, the central region, which included the city of Jerusalem, was specifically designated for the descendants of Shem.

So, in both the accounts of Moses and Joshua, we see a profound connection between the historical journey of the Israelites, their rightful and divine inheritance of Canaan, and the enduring significance of Noah's division of land among his descendants.

Joshua's mandate to conquer the land and dispossess its inhabitants must be viewed in the context of correcting the disobedience and unlawful occupation symbolized by Canaan's actions many centuries prior. Joshua's directives were not merely about conquest; they were a response to God's mandate and the belief in the divine obligation for the children of Israel to claim the land allotted to their forefather, Shem. This was an endeavor to fulfill the divine plan articulated by Noah.

Joshua 10:41-42:
"Joshua subdued them from Kadesh Barnea to Gaza and from the whole region of Goshen to Gibeon. All these kings and their lands Joshua conquered in one campaign because the Lord, the God of Israel, fought for Israel."

While the commands and actions led by Joshua may seem harsh at first glance, they were considered necessary to correct the legacy of past disobedience and, more importantly, to fulfill God's promises to the descendants of Shem, particularly the seed of Abraham, the children of Israel. This scenario reflects a complex dynamic of divine authority, obedience, and the reestablishment of God's intended order in the Promised Land. Additionally, the brothers had committed themselves to an oath, imposing an eternal curse on anyone who dared to overstep their divinely allotted portion of land, as determined by the casting of lots.

The actions of Joshua were motivated because of the oath sworn about 1500 years earlier. Central to this oath was a stern warning—a curse pronounced on anyone who dared to seize a portion of land not allotted to them by the casting of lots. The gravity of this curse cannot be overstated, for it carried not only earthly consequences but spiritual ones as well.

The sons of Noah, recognizing the profound import of this oath, responded in unison, declaring, *"So be it; so be it."* This collective affirmation echoed through the ages, binding their commitment to the oath and extending its authority throughout all generations.

Crucially, this solemn oath encompassed a vision of the future—a day of judgment ordained by the Lord God. This day, as foreseen by Noah, would be characterized by divine reckoning, where God's judgment would be executed with a sword and with fire. It would serve as retribution for the unclean wickedness, errors, transgressions, uncleanness, fornication, and sin that had marred the earth.

In essence, the oath encapsulated the moral and spiritual compass by which Noah's descendants were to navigate their existence. It was a covenant that affirmed their commitment to uphold the divine order, respect the boundaries of their allotted lands, and live in accordance with God's divine plan. Disobedience to this covenant was not merely a violation of land rights; it was a challenge to divine authority and a disruption of the harmonious order established by God through Noah.

The oath, with its curses and the looming day of judgment, served as a timeless reminder to humanity—a reminder of the solemn promises made, the consequences of transgression, and the enduring importance of adhering to divine decrees. It was a sacred thread that connected generations, fostering an understanding of their responsibilities to God's divine plan, as entrusted to them by their forefather, Noah.

The story encapsulating Canaan's disobedience and Joshua's command to conquer the land occupied by Canaanites weaves together intricate themes of divine authority, obedience, and the fulfillment of God's promises to specific lineages. It offers profound insights into the consequences of disobedience and the ultimate restoration of divine order in the context of the area called "Promised Land.

In this solemn covenant, Noah, as the patriarch of his family, bound all of his sons by an unbreakable oath. This oath was no ordinary commitment; it was a pact sealed with divine significance. It bore witness to their acceptance of their designated territories and the divine order decreed by God.

Joshua's campaign in the land of Canaan is one of the most debated and discussed events in the biblical narrative. To understand the justification for his actions, it is crucial to delve into the historical and theological context, mainly as presented in the Bible and the Book of Jubilees.

Fulfillment of God's Promise:
The portion of land fell to Shem and his descendants in lots for eternity.

God promised Abraham that his descendants would inherit the land of Canaan (Genesis 12:7, 15:18-21). This promise was reiterated to Isaac (Genesis 26:3) and Jacob (Genesis 28:13). Joshua's conquest fulfilled this divine promise.

The Book of Jubilees and the Divine Mandate:

The Book of Jubilees, an ancient Jewish text, expounds further on this narrative. It emphasizes that the Canaanites were living in the land illegitimately. According to Jubilees 10:29-34, Canaan transgressed when he learned from Noah about the division of the land and then chose to settle in the Eastern portion, which was not his designated territory. This encroachment was an act of disobedience, and the Canaanites' presence in the land was viewed as unlawful from all of his brothers and the divine mandate given to them.

The Oath and Divine Reckoning:

The Book of Jubilees (particularly in chapter 5) speaks of the sins of humanity leading to the flood and the subsequent division of the earth among Noah's sons. Canaan's seizure of some of the land led to a pronounced curse (Jubilees 10:30-33). Joshua's actions can be seen as the implementation of this oath and the fulfillment of the divine reckoning.

Joshua's conquest of Canaan was not an arbitrary act of aggression. From the perspective of the biblical narrative and the Book of Jubilees, it was the fulfillment of a divine promise and mandate, an act of judgment against the wickedness of the Canaanites, and a preventive measure against the spiritual contamination of Israel. The various scriptures and references provide a multifaceted justification rooted deeply in the religious, historical, and moral context of the time.

The Oath and Divine Reckoning:

Within the framework of the Book of Jubilees, the significance of oaths and their implications are profound. Particularly in chapter 5, the text delves into the prehistoric world's wickedness, culminating in the catastrophic flood. Following the flood, Noah divides the earth among his sons, and it is during this division that Canaan's aforementioned transgression occurs. Due to Canaan's disobedience, a curse is pronounced (as mentioned in Jubilees 10:30-33). This curse not only denotes a temporal punishment but also foreshadows a divine reckoning that would span generations. Joshua's military campaign against the Canaanites can be perceived within this context. His actions were not just a military conquest but also represented the manifestation of the oath's weight and the onset of the divine reckoning long foretold.

The Exile to the Return

The Babylonian Exile represents one of the most defining epochs in the extensive history of the Children of Israel. This event wasn't just a geographical dislocation; it was a profound spiritual and cultural upheaval that left an indelible mark on Jewish identity, spirituality, and theological perspectives.

Several interwoven factors precipitated this exile. Foremost was religious apostasy. Over time, the Children of Israel, particularly those in positions of influence in Jerusalem, gradually shifted away from the monotheistic worship of Yahweh. Seduced by the religious practices of surrounding civilizations, they embraced idol worship, a stark violation of their sacred covenant with God.

Additionally, political misjudgments played a crucial role. The kings of Judah, in their attempts to assert autonomy, often made politically expedient decisions that antagonized their overlords. Aligning with Egypt and rebelling against the Babylonian Empire were strategic missteps that invited retribution.

The internal fabric of Israelite society was also fraying. Prophets, the moral compass of the society, continuously raised alarms about the widening socioeconomic disparities. The affluent classes were increasingly marginalizing the underprivileged, creating an environment rife with injustice.

Amid these societal shifts, voices of caution emerged. Prophets such as Jeremiah, Isaiah, and Ezekiel sounded clarion calls for repentance, warning of impending doom if the nation continued on its perilous path. Yet, their admonitions were largely ignored.

The culmination of these tensions was the siege of Jerusalem by Nebuchadnezzar II, the Babylonian king, around 587/586 BCE. The subsequent fall of this revered city was cataclysmic. The destruction of Solomon's Temple, an emblem of God's presence, epitomized this tragedy. The societal elite, including royalty, priests, and intellectuals, were forcibly relocated to Babylon, marking the onset of a 70-year exile.[i]

Yet, in these depths of despair, a glimmer of hope persisted. The same prophets who warned of the exile also spoke of redemption. Isaiah and Jeremiah, among others, prophesied a time of divine intervention, where God would guide His people back to their homeland. They envisioned a renewed Israel, where the land would once again flourish, and the people, under a new covenant, would rebuild the temple, reestablishing their sacred bond with the Almighty.

This prophecy materialized when geopolitical dynamics shifted. The emerging Persian Empire, under the astute leadership of Cyrus the Great, vanquished the Babylonians. In a historic decree around 538 BCE, Cyrus authorized the return of the Israelites. This homecoming unfolded in distinct phases:

Sheshbazzar's Leadership (538 BCE): A pioneering group led by Prince Sheshbazzar of Judah embarked on the journey back and began constructing the Second Temple. (Briant)

Zerubbabel's Era (c. 520-515 BCE): With Zerubbabel at the helm and inspired by prophets Haggai and Zechariah, the Second Temple was brought to completion.[13]

Ezra's Reforms (c. 458 BCE): Ezra, a learned scribe, ushered in an era emphasizing religious purity and a renewed commitment to the Torah.[14]

Nehemiah's Endeavors (c. 445 BCE): Nehemiah's leadership focused on physically fortifying Jerusalem by rebuilding its walls and spiritually revitalizing its populace.[15]

In retrospect, while the Babylonian Exile was undoubtedly a period of anguish for the Children of Israel, it also served as a crucible for their faith. The experience reinforced their monotheistic beliefs, deepened their reverence for the Torah, and strengthened their collective identity. Their triumphant return from exile is not just a testament to God's unwavering promises but also a reflection of the enduring spirit and resilience of the Jewish people.

---

13   Ezra 2:2 and Ezra 3:2-8.

14   Ezra 7 -10.

15   Nehemiah 1

From the Romans to 1948, the state of Israel

The Second Exile and Return: From Roman Destruction to the Establishment of the State of Israel

During the first century AD, Judea found itself subjugated under the vast dominion of the Roman Empire. This transition of power came after the region had experienced the influence of the Hellenistic Seleucids[16] and had been governed by the Jewish Hasmonean dynasty. As time unfolded, the relationship between the Jewish inhabitants of Judea and their Roman overlords became increasingly strained. This mounting tension was a product of deep-rooted cultural and religious disparities that existed between the two groups. Moreover, the policies imposed by the Roman administration, which often seemed arbitrary or insensitive to Jewish customs and beliefs, further exacerbated these tensions, setting the stage for significant conflicts in the years to come.

The Great Revolt (66-70 AD):

In 66 AD, simmering resentments in Judea reached a boiling point. Fueled by mounting frustrations over Roman mandates and impositions, the Jewish community in Judea took a stand, igniting what would be remembered as the First Jewish-Roman War or, more commonly, the Great Revolt. Initially, the Jewish rebels managed to gain some notable victories, bolstering their confidence and resilience. However, as the Romans rallied their vast military might, the tide of the conflict began to turn against

---

16   The Seleucids were a Hellenistic dynasty that ruled over a significant portion of the eastern part of Alexander the Great's former empire after his death in the 4th century BCE.

the rebels. This prolonged struggle culminated in a tragic climax in 70 AD when the Roman legions, led by the future Emperor Titus, breached the walls of Jerusalem. The city endured a devastating siege, leading to widespread destruction and loss of life. One of the most grievous casualties of this siege was the Second Temple, a beacon of Jewish faith and identity, which was razed to the ground by the Roman forces. This event not only marked the end of the revolt but also signified a profound loss for the Jewish people, both spiritually and culturally. (Josephus)

Destruction of the Second Temple (70 AD):

In 70 AD, under the relentless pressure of a siege directed by the Roman general Titus, Jerusalem's defenses finally crumbled. The Roman legions, renowned for their military precision and ruthlessness, poured into the city. As they sought control and dominance, they left a trail of devastation in their wake. However, the most profound blow to the Jewish people during this conquest was the deliberate destruction of the Second Temple. This monumental structure wasn't just an architectural marvel; it stood as the epicenter of Jewish spiritual, religious, and cultural identity. For generations, it had been where the Jewish community congregated for major religious observances, offered sacrifices and sought spiritual solace. Its destruction was, therefore, not merely a tactical victory for the Romans but a strategic move to dismantle the very soul of Jewish existence. The loss of the Temple sent ripples of grief, confusion, and disorientation across the Jewish diaspora, marking an end to an era and the beginning of a new phase of Jewish history, one characterized by diasporic existence, adaptation, and a deep yearning for return.

The Diaspora:

The cataclysmic events of 70 AD, culminating in the fall of Jerusalem and the obliteration of the Second Temple, set the stage for a profound transformation in Jewish history: the onset of the diaspora. As the Roman legions asserted their dominance, the repercussions were felt deeply by the Jewish populace. Thousands met tragic deaths, either in the brutalities of war or in its grim aftermath. Additionally, many found themselves shackled and transported to various corners of the Roman Empire, condemned to a life of servitude and slavery. Yet, there were also those who, sensing the impending doom or in the chaos that followed, made the heart-wrenching decision to leave their homeland. They journeyed to diverse regions within the expansive Roman territories and even ventured beyond its borders. As they settled in new lands, these Jewish communities faced the challenge of preserving their unique religious and cultural identity amidst foreign influences. Over time, they established synagogues, schools, and community centers, ensuring the continuity of Jewish traditions and practices. This widespread dispersion of the Jewish people, triggered by the tragic events in Jerusalem, marked the dawn of an enduring diaspora, shaping the course of Jewish history and identity for centuries to come.

Bar Kokhba Revolt (132-135 AD):

In 132 AD, the embers of resistance against Roman domination were rekindled, giving rise to the Bar Kokhba Revolt. Under the leadership of Simon Bar Kokhba, who was viewed by many as the Messiah, the Jewish community in Judea mounted a formidable challenge against their Roman overlords. For a brief period, it appeared the rebels might indeed rewrite the annals of history. The revolt witnessed initial successes, with the rebels reclaiming considerable territories and even minting their own coins. However, the Roman Empire, with its vast military resources, was not to be subdued easily.

By 135 AD, under the determined leadership of Emperor Hadrian, the Romans systematically crushed the revolt, inflicting immense casualties on the Jewish population. The aftermath of this failed uprising was dire for the Jews. Not only were they met with severe persecution, but they were also forbidden from entering Jerusalem, effectively alienating them from the spiritual heartland that had defined their identity for centuries. This decree further entrenched the Jewish diaspora, as more Jews sought refuge in lands far from the epicenter of their agonizing defeat. The Bar Kokhba Revolt, while emblematic of the indomitable Jewish spirit, also marked a pivotal moment in Jewish history, deepening the chasm between the Jewish people and their ancestral homeland. (Powell)

Diaspora Life:
Throughout the long span of history following the destruction of Jerusalem and the consequential upheavals against Roman dominion, Jewish diaspora communities found themselves laying roots in a multitude of areas ranging from the Iberian Peninsula in Western Europe through the diverse terrains of Central Europe to the sands of North Africa, and the ancient landscapes of Mesopotamia in the Middle East. Within these diverse geographical terrains and amidst various host cultures, the Jewish diaspora displayed remarkable tenacity and adaptability.

These communities, while embracing certain aspects of their host cultures, ensured the safeguarding of their unique identity. Preserving their identity wasn't just a passive act; it required active and continuous effort. Synagogues, which served as places of worship and community gathering, sprouted up in cities and villages, becoming centers of learning and debate. The rigorous study of the Torah, the Talmud, and other religious texts became pivotal in keeping the community anchored to its roots. Life cycle events, such as births, marriages, and deaths, were marked by age-old rituals that served as a testament to the community's endurance and commitment to tradition.

Furthermore, an ever-present nostalgia for Zion[17], their ancestral land, was deeply embedded in the Jewish psyche. This was not just an abstract or romanticized notion; it manifested in daily prayers, annual observances like Tisha B'Av (which mourned the destruction of the First and Second Temples), and the famous Passover declaration, "Next year in Jerusalem." This perpetual yearning was more than just a memory; it became a beacon of hope and resilience. Even as centuries rolled by and generations were born in foreign lands, the collective memory of their homeland remained undiminished. This deep-seated longing underscored the diaspora experience, serving as a testament to the unbreakable bond between people and their historical homeland.

---

17   In the Hebrew Bible (Old Testament), "Zion" typically refers to a specific hill in Jerusalem, also known as Mount Zion. It is often used metaphorically to symbolize Jerusalem or the entire Promised Land.

The Oath and the Jewish Diaspora:
Exploring Historical Linkages

The cataclysmic event of the Second Temple's demolition by the Romans in 70 CE marked a turning point in Jewish history, culminating in their vast dispersion. Known as the Diaspora, this migration led many Jews to establish European communities, notably in regions traditionally linked to Japheth's lineage. The movement of the Jewish populace across various global territories forms an integral narrative within Jewish chronicles. A notable theory, intertwined with the oath sworn by Noah's progeny — Shem, Ham, and Japheth — postulates that the Jewish habitation in European domains, especially those tied to Japheth, might bear significant historical and theological ramifications. Let's delve into this intriguing viewpoint:

The Oath:

Building upon the biblical premise established with Canaan, one might postulate whether the Jewish diaspora in Europe could be linked to a similar dynamic. Given that the descendants of Japheth were designated to occupy territories in Europe and parts of Asia, the extensive Jewish settlement in European lands could, through a rigid scriptural lens, be perceived as a deviation from the divine territorial allocation.

Drawing from the Canaan narrative, where transgressing territorial bounds led to a curse, it is tempting to speculate whether the hardships and persecutions faced by Jews in Europe over the centuries could be understood as repercussions of a similar curse. Such a perspective suggests that the Jewish community's challenges in Europe might be intertwined with their residence outside of the territories that were biblically designated to their lineage. However, it's essential to approach this hypothesis with caution and sensitivity, recognizing the myriad factors that have influenced Jewish history and the potential dangers of oversimplifying complex socio-political events through a singular theological lens.

Persecution in Europe:

Over the centuries, Jews faced persecution in various European territories. Events such as pogroms[ii], the Spanish Inquisition, and the Holocaust in Nazi Germany were significant tragedies that affected the Jewish community. Could this persecution be linked to the violation of the territorial oath? Some argue that settling in Japheth's territories may have upset a divine balance, leading to continuous unrest and persecution.

Counterarguments:

However, the theory that links the Jewish Diaspora to an oath taken by Shem, Ham, and Japheth is met with various counterarguments, chief among them being the nature of the diaspora itself. The dispersion of the Jews was not a voluntary migration driven by a collective desire to venture into new territories. Instead, it was precipitated by a series of forced expulsions, severe persecutions, and tragic events that spanned centuries. In light of these circumstances, one could contend that the Jewish people, faced with existential threats, were left with little choice but to seek refuge wherever possible. Their movement across continents was a desperate quest for survival, safety, and a life free from relentless persecution. The essence of their journey was not to infringe upon an ancient oath but was a testament to their indomitable spirit and will to persevere against overwhelming odds.

In concluding this discussion, it's pivotal to emphasize that while the oath of Shem, Ham, and Japheth offers an intriguing perspective on Jewish history, it represents merely one angle of interpretation. Jewish historical experiences are profoundly intricate, shaped by a myriad of events and interpretations, rendering it an oversimplification to ascribe them to a singular cause or theory. Central to this complexity is the undeniable fact that the diaspora wasn't an act of choice or voluntary migration. It was, in essence, a dire consequence of relentless forced expulsions and brutal persecutions. Thus, the overarching narrative of the Jewish people during this period is not one of intentional territorial expansion but of a resilient community persistently seeking refuge, safety, and a beacon of hope amidst adversity. I don't have the answer, but it is something to consider.

The Hope of Returning Home

Throughout the annals of history, there exists a consistent and powerful motif that has defined the human experience: the yearning for home. This longing, which transcends boundaries and generations, finds profound resonance in the Biblical narrative of the children of Israel. The story of their exile and the promise of their return home paints a poignant portrait of hope, faith, and divine intervention.

Amid their struggles and moments of despair, the words of the prophets served as a beacon of light. The prophet Jeremiah, for instance, conveyed God's assurance: "Behold, I will gather them out of all countries where I have driven them... and I will bring them back to this place, and I will cause them to dwell safely" (Jeremiah 32:37). This wasn't just a promise of a physical return, but an emotional and spiritual homecoming as well.

Isaiah's poetic eloquence reinforced this hope, proclaiming: "I will bring your children from the east and gather you from the west... Bring my sons from afar and my daughters from the ends of the earth" (Isaiah 43:5-7). The sweeping vision of families reuniting, of children born in foreign lands returning to their ancestral grounds, was not merely a future prediction but a clarion call to trust in the enduring covenant between God and His people.

Ezekiel, too, rekindled this hope. In his vision, he spoke of God's intention to bring the Israelites from all corners, making them "one nation in the land, on the mountains of Israel" (Ezekiel 37:21-23). Beyond just a return to territory, this was a promise of unity, of a collective identity reborn and strengthened.

The longing to return to their ancestral land, as described in these scriptures, goes beyond a simple change of location. It's a return to a sacred homeland bestowed upon their ancestor Shem nearly 4,167 years earlier. This return symbolizes a deeper journey to one's roots, the core of personal identity, and most importantly, a reestablishment of connection with the divine guardianship of YHWH. It epitomizes the resilient human spirit that endures even in the darkest times, holding onto the hope for a brighter future. In this enduring story, individuals can find reflections of their own longing, hopes, and pursuit of a place where they truly belong.

The promise that God will return the descendants of Shem to their land and ensure they are never uprooted again can be found in several places in the Bible. One of the most prominent references is in the Book of Amos:

"But I will plant them upon their soil, **nevermore** to be uprooted from the soil I have given them — said the LORD your God." - Amos 9:15

This verse comes after God promises to restore the fallen 'booth of David' and to bring the exiles of Israel back from captivity. The assurance in this passage underscores the eternal covenant between God and the people of Israel, the descendants of Shem.

Amos 9:15.
"But I will plant them upon their soil, nevermore to be uprooted from the soil I have given them — said the LORD your God."

Jeremiah 32:37-41:
"Behold, I will gather them out of all countries where I have driven them in my anger, and in my fury, and in great wrath; and I will bring them back to this place, and I will cause them to dwell safely: And they shall be my people, and I will be their God. I will give them one heart and one way, that they may fear me forever, for their own good and the good of their children after them. I will make an everlasting covenant with them, never turning away from doing good to them..."

Isaiah 43:5-7:
"Do not be afraid, for I am with you; I will bring your children from the east and gather you from the west. I will say to the north, 'Give them up!' and to the south, 'Do not hold them back.' Bring

my sons from afar and my daughters from the ends of the earth—everyone who is called by my name, whom I created for my glory, whom I formed and made."

Ezekiel 37:21-23:

"Thus says the Lord GOD: Behold, I will take the people of Israel from the nations among which they have gone, and will gather them from all sides and bring them to their own land; and I will make them one nation in the land, on the mountains of Israel. They shall not defile themselves anymore with their idols and their detestable things, or with any of their transgressions..."

Prophecy Fulfilled: The Zionist Movement and the Return

Throughout the vast and intricate tapestry of human history, there have been numerous instances where current events appear to resonate profoundly with the ancient prophecies of bygone eras. A striking example of this phenomenon can be observed in the emergence and development of the Zionist movement during the late 19th and early 20th centuries. This movement, which advocated for the establishment of a Jewish homeland, seems almost to mirror the foretellings found in ancient texts.

The Zionist movement's inception, growth, and eventual success in establishing a nation state in what is now Israel, stand as a remarkable testament to the dynamic interplay between ancient prophecy and its fulfillment. This intriguing dance of destiny and intention showcases how visions of the past can shape and inspire the realities of the future, creating a narrative thread that weaves through the fabric of time.

Birth of Zionism:

As the 19th century waned, Europe was in the throes of significant socio-political transformations. Nationalist sentiments were sweeping across nations, redefining borders and identities. Against this backdrop emerged the Zionist movement, deeply rooted in the millennia-old Jewish connection to the land of Israel. While the idea of returning to Zion had always been a cornerstone of Jewish prayer and identity, the emergence of modern Zionism transformed this spiritual yearning into a tangible political and social mission.

The sparks that ignited this movement were manifold. Increasing anti-Semitic incidents, notably the Dreyfus affair[18] in France and pogroms in Russia served as grim reminders of the precarious position of Jewish communities in Europe. These events, coupled with the stirring writings of visionaries like Theodor Herzl, catalyzed a collective awakening. Herzl's seminal work, "The Jewish State," envisioned the establishment of a sovereign Jewish state as the only viable solution to the 'Jewish Question' — the enduring challenges faced by Jews in the diaspora.

It was not just about a refuge from persecution. Zionism, at its heart, was about reclamation — of land, of identity, and of destiny. It resonated with the age-old biblical promises, where prophets like Isaiah and Jeremiah spoke of a grand return to Zion. The Zionist Congresses, beginning in 1897, became platforms for Jews worldwide to congregate, strategize, and dream of a homeland.

---

18   The Dreyfus Affair was a pivotal 19th-century French scandal involving the wrongful conviction of Jewish Army Captain Alfred Dreyfus for treason, highlighting deep societal divisions and influencing the rise of Zionism

They discussed practical steps, from purchasing land in Palestine to promoting Hebrew as a modern, living language.

By the time the 20th century dawned, the Zionist vision was no longer a distant dream. Jewish pioneers, or 'halutzim,' began arriving in Palestine, laying the groundwork for the state-to-be. They established settlements, revived Hebrew as a spoken language, and set up cultural, educational, and economic institutions.

In the annals of history, the Zionist movement stands as a powerful embodiment of prophecy realized. It symbolizes the indomitable spirit of a people who, driven by faith and historical memory, sought to shape their own destiny. In their journey, one can see the reflections of ancient prophecies and, in their achievements, the fulfillment of age-old aspirations.

FROM THE BIRTH OF ZIONISM TO THE BALFOUR DECLARATION:

The rise of the Zionist movement in the late 19th and early 20th centuries and the eventual issuance of the Balfour Declaration in 1917 are not isolated events but interlinked stages of a broader historical narrative. The dream of establishing a Jewish homeland, influenced by diverse forces and events, would reach a pivotal moment with the British government's endorsement.

The Emergence of Modern Zionism:

The origins of the Zionist movement can be traced back to the late 19th century, with figures like Theodor Herzl advocating for the establishment of a Jewish homeland as a response to growing anti-Semitism in Europe. The First Zionist Congress in 1897 in Basel, Switzerland, officially marked the start of the political Zionist endeavor.

Diplomatic Efforts:

Key Zionist leaders understood the importance of international support. Chaim Weizmann, who would later become Israel's first president, was particularly active in Britain, forging relationships with influential figures in the political and intellectual circles.

World War I and the Ottoman Empire:

The geopolitical landscape shifted dramatically during World War I. The Ottoman Empire, which had controlled Palestine for centuries, was in decline and sided with the Central Powers. As the war progressed, the Allied Powers, including Britain, saw an opportunity to influence the future of the Middle East should they emerge victorious.

Britain's Strategic Interests:

For Britain, control over Palestine had strategic value, serving as a bridge to its colonial interests in India and the East. There was also sympathy and support for the Zionist cause within the British establishment. Leaders like David Lloyd George and Lord Arthur Balfour were, for various reasons, amenable to the idea of a Jewish homeland in Palestine.

The Balfour Declaration:

In this context, on November 2, 1917, the British Foreign Secretary, Arthur James Balfour, sent a letter to Lord Walter Rothschild, a leading British Jew and Zionist, declaring the British government's support for the establishment of a "national home for the Jewish people" in Palestine. This became known as the Balfour Declaration. It's worth noting that the declaration did emphasize that "nothing shall be done which may prejudice the civil and religious rights of existing non-Jewish communities in Palestine."

The Balfour Declaration did not materialize out of thin air. It resulted from years of lobbying by Zionist leaders, geopolitical shifts due to World War I, and the strategic interests of the British Empire. While the declaration itself did not create a Jewish state, it provided the Zionist movement with a significant boost and an internationally recognized endorsement that would pave the way for the eventual establishment of the State of Israel in 1948.

THE BRITISH MANDATE OF PALESTINE (1920-1948): A PERIOD OF TRANSITION AND TUMULT

The British Mandate of Palestine, spanning nearly three decades, was a pivotal chapter in the history of the Middle East. It was a period marked by nationalistic aspirations, geopolitical maneuvers, and the deepening of communal divides. The backdrop of the mandate era was an intricate interplay between British colonial interests, Jewish Zionist aspirations, and Arab nationalism.

Establishing the Mandate:

After the end of World War I, the League of Nations, to reorganize territories previously under the Ottoman Empire, granted Britain the mandate to govern Palestine in 1922. The mandate incorporated the Balfour Declaration, committing Britain to the establishment of a "national home for the Jewish people" in Palestine while ensuring that the rights of other communities were not prejudiced.

Jewish Immigration and Settlement:

With the protective umbrella of the British administration, Jewish immigration to Palestine increased significantly. Many were fleeing persecution from Europe, particularly after the rise of Nazism in the 1930s. They bought land, set up agricultural settlements, and began building the institutional foundations of a future state. The Jewish Agency played a pivotal role in facilitating immigration and settlement.

Arab Concerns and Opposition:

The increased Jewish immigration and land purchases raised concerns among the Arab majority. They felt increasingly marginalized in their "own homeland." This led to tensions, resulting in sporadic outbreaks of violence against both the Jewish immigrants and the British administration. The Arab Revolt of 1936-1939 was a notable manifestation of this opposition.

British Policy and the White Papers:

To balance its commitments to both Jewish and Arab communities, Britain released several policy documents known as White Papers. The most significant, issued in 1939, aimed to limit Jewish immigration and land purchases, envisioning an independent Palestine governed jointly by Jews and Arabs within ten years. This policy responded to Arab concerns but was met with strong opposition from the Zionist movement.

World War II and its Aftermath:

The horrors of the Holocaust intensified the urgency for a Jewish homeland. Survivors of the genocide sought refuge in Palestine, but many were turned away or interned by the British due to their immigration policies. This led to growing Jewish resistance against British rule. Groups like the Haganah, Irgun, and Lehi operated against British forces.

The Road to Partition:

By the late 1940s, with tensions escalating and Britain unable to devise a satisfactory solution, the issue of Palestine was handed over to the newly formed United Nations. In 1947, the UN proposed the partition of Palestine into separate Jewish and Arab states with an international administration for Jerusalem. Despite Jewish acceptance, the plan was rejected by the Arab nations.

End of the Mandate and Birth of Israel:

In 1948, Britain officially ended its mandate, leading to the declaration of the State of Israel by David Ben-Gurion. This was immediately followed by the 1948 Arab-Israeli War, with neighboring Arab countries invading the newly declared state.

In essence, the British Mandate of Palestine was a crucible of competing nationalisms. The legacy of this period, marked by both cooperation and conflict, continues to shape the politics and narratives of the region.

Establishment of the State of Israel:

UN Partition Plan (1947):

In the aftermath of World War II and the Holocaust, there was a heightened urgency to address the Jewish refugee crisis and the long-standing Jewish national aspirations. The British, who held the mandate over Palestine since the end of World War I, faced growing tensions and conflicts between Jewish immigrants, who were increasing in numbers due to the persecution they faced in Europe, and the Arab residents who had lived there for centuries. Unable to find a sustainable solution, the British handed the issue over to the newly formed United Nations in 1947.

The United Nations Special Committee on Palestine (UNSCOP) was formed to examine the issue and propose solutions. After thorough deliberations, the committee recommended the partition of Palestine into separate Jewish and Arab states. The proposal was driven by a recognition of the historical connection of Jews to the region, the weight of their recent sufferings, and the aspirations of the Zionist movement. At the same time, the rights of the Arab majority residing in the area were also considered, leading to the recommendation of an independent Arab state.

On November 29, 1947, the United Nations General Assembly adopted the partition plan as Resolution 181. The plan proposed dividing the territory into three entities: a Jewish state, an Arab state, and an international administration for Jerusalem, given its religious significance to Jews, Christians, and Muslims alike.

The Jewish Agency for Palestine accepted the partition plan, and they declared the establishment of the State of Israel on May 14, 1948. However, the Arab nations and Palestinian Arab leadership rejected the UN proposal, leading to the 1948 Arab-Israeli war, marking the beginning of a series of conflicts in the region.

> *"Who hath heard such a thing? Who hath seen such things?*
> *Shall the earth be made to bring forth in one day? or shall*
> *a nation be born at once? For as soon as Zion travailed, she*
> *brought forth her children."*
> *— Isaiah 66:8*

Declaration of the State of Israel (1948):

The words from Isaiah 66:8 are hauntingly prophetic, posing the question: "Who hath heard such a thing? who hath seen such things?" It speaks of the unparalleled event where the earth witnesses the birth of a nation in a single day, a phenomenon that seems almost unimaginable. The verse alludes to Zion's labor pains, suggesting a period of intense struggle and adversity, but it also promises a rewarding outcome: "As soon as Zion travailed, she brought forth her children."

Fast forward to May 14, 1948, a date forever etched in the annals of history. The dream of a Jewish homeland, nurtured for centuries, was on the cusp of becoming a reality. David Ben-Gurion, leading the World Zionist Organization and chairing the Jewish Agency for Palestine, took center stage in Tel Aviv to make a proclamation that would change the course of history: the birth of the State of Israel. This wasn't just a sudden, spontaneous announcement; it was the climax of years of relentless Zionist endeavors, strategic planning, and an unwavering determination to reestablish a Jewish state in the land of their forefathers.

As the clock ticked to the end of the British Mandate, Ben-Gurion, with great reverence, acknowledged the deep-seated, millennia-old connection the Jewish people held with this land. He did not just speak of ancient ties; he also touched upon the more recent, painful memories, most poignantly the Holocaust's atrocities. In his vision for the new state, Ben-Gurion envisaged a society that embodied the ideals of liberty, justice, and peace, echoing the teachings of the Hebrew prophets.

Yet, as with many monumental historical moments, this euphoria was fleeting. Almost immediately, on May 15, 1948, the newborn state faced an existential threat. A coalition of Arab forces, including troops from Egypt, Transjordan, Syria, Iraq, and Lebanon, mounted a military offensive against Israel. Their goal was clear: to challenge the legitimacy of Israel and halt its very existence. This confrontation marked the onset of the 1948 Arab-Israeli War, referred to by Israelis as the War of Independence. It was the first chapter in a long, intricate narrative of geopolitical tensions in the Middle East, with the Israeli-Palestinian conflict at its heart.

Endurance, Resilience, and Renaissance:

In the annals of history, Israel stands out as a testament to the power of endurance and the strength of collective will. Amidst the initial adversities faced during its inception, the young nation displayed exceptional determination. Instead of merely surviving the odds, Israel demonstrated an ability to adapt, evolve, and ultimately expand its territories.

Over subsequent years, this resilience was further highlighted by the mass influx of Jewish immigrants. These weren't mere migrations; they represented profound journeys filled with hope and purpose. From distant lands and diverse cultures, Jews converged upon Israel, marking a reunion with their ancestral home. This significant movement served as a symbolic reconnection, bridging the long chasm of a nearly 2,000-year exile.

The return to Israel was not merely a matter of geography or politics; it was the embodiment of ancient scriptures and prophecies manifesting in the modern era. As these scriptures foretold, the children of Abraham were reclaiming their covenantal land—a divine pact linking them to this specific stretch of land. This narrative gains even more depth considering the ties to Shem, an ancestor revered in Jewish tradition. According to these traditions, the land that modern-day Israelis were settling had been predestined for Shem's lineage.

Final Reflection:

The journey of the Jewish people, marked by a second exile followed by a triumphant return leading to the creation of the State of Israel, stands as an unparalleled narrative of tenacity, adaptability, and unyielding spirit. From the catastrophic events of 70 AD, which saw the obliteration of their sacred spaces, to the monumental re-founding of their national homeland in 1948, their odyssey is more than just a series of historical events. It is a chronicle filled with lessons of perseverance, hope, and the unwavering belief in a brighter future. This enduring saga, etched in the annals of time, serves as a beacon, illuminating the capabilities of humanity when faced with seemingly insurmountable challenges.

CHAPTER 7

∽༠∾

"I always said that in our war with the Arabs, we had a secret weapon - no alternative."
Benjamin Netanyahu

BENJAMIN AND THE PALESTINIAN PEOPLE

The Middle East today is a landscape deeply scarred by strife and conflict, notably epitomized by the intense hostilities between Israel and Hamas within the Palestinian territories. Although these confrontations are frequently analyzed through a modern perspective, they are deeply rooted in historical events. The narrative stretches back to ancient times, including significant moments such as Abraham's involvement in the Battle of the Kings and Joshua's military campaigns in Gaza, which set the stage for the contemporary clash between Israel and Hamas.

These historical roots of the conflict, especially in the territories of Gaza and Israel, are intricately woven with religious and historical narratives. Among these is the story of Noah's sons—Shem, Ham, and Japheth—who, as described in ancient scriptures, divided the world among their descendants after the Great Flood. In this process, Canaan, in violation of the established oath, settled in lands not designated to him and his descendants, sowing the seeds of longstanding territorial disputes.

Following this narrative, the Canaanites—descendants of Ham—are viewed as having settled in territories that were not their designated allotment, breaching this sacred oath. Such a perceived transgression laid the groundwork for the subsequent Israelite conquest of Canaan. In this historical context, the Israelites, stemming from the lineage of Shem, regarded their actions as a reclamation of their divinely ordained inheritance.

In the present context, some interpret the Palestinian presence and territorial claims as reminiscent of the Canaanites' ancient transgression. This viewpoint likens the Palestinians to the Canaanites, suggesting they inhabit lands traditionally believed to be divinely allocated to the descendants of Shem. This interpretation implies that the current challenges of the Palestinians parallel the biblical fate of the Canaanites. This historical parallel draws on the scriptural curse, as expressed in the words of Ham, Cush, and Mizraim to their brother Canaan: **"Thou hast settled in a land which is not thine, and which did not fall to us by lot: do not do so; for if thou dost do so, thou and thy sons will fall in the land and be accursed through sedition; for by sedition ye have settled, and by sedition will thy children fall, and thou shalt be rooted out forever."**

ORIGIN OF THE PALESTINIAN PEOPLE

The region known as Palestine has been inhabited for millennia by various ancient peoples, including the Canaanites, Jebusites, and Philistines. The Israelites settled here after their Exodus from Egypt, and the area saw control by empires like the Babylonians, Persians, Greeks, and Romans. In the 7th century AD, Muslim Arab armies introduced Islam, and most locals converted. The area changed hands between various rulers, including the Crusaders, Mamluks, and Ottomans. A distinct Palestinian identity formed during the Ottoman era further shaped under British control after World War I. The end of British rule in 1948 led to the declaration of Israel and subsequent conflicts. Today's Palestinians are mainly Arab, speaking Arabic and predominantly practicing Islam, with a shared history and strong connection to the land and descendants of the Canaanites.

THE OTTOMAN EMPIRE AND THE ARAB SETTLEMENT IN PALESTINE

The Ottoman Empire, which lasted from 1299 to 1922 at its zenith, stretched from the Persian Gulf in the east to Algeria in the west. Palestine, a region on the eastern coast of the Mediterranean Sea, was under Ottoman rule from 1517 to 1917.

Ottoman Administrative Structure and Policies in Palestine: Palestine's administrative division during the early Ottoman period was initially part of the Damascus Eyalet (province). Later, it was divided into several Sanjaks (districts) like Jerusalem, Gaza, and Nablus. The Ottoman administration brought relative stability and prosperity to the region, which benefited agriculture and trade.

Migration and Settlement Policies: One of the cornerstones of the Ottoman administrative system was the land tenure system. Lands were categorized under several titles, and a significant portion was state land. To optimize tax revenues and ensure effective military conscription, the empire encouraged the sedentarization of nomadic populations and sometimes relocated populations for administrative convenience.

Tanzimat Reforms:

Initiated in the mid-19th century, these reforms aimed to modernize the empire and consolidate central authority. As part of these reforms, land legislation was introduced, prompting many landowners to register communal lands in their names. This often led to Arab peasants (fellahin) working on lands technically owned by absentee landlords, many of whom lived in cities like Beirut or Damascus. The peasants, in many cases, were unaware of this ownership change and continued their daily life, farming lands their ancestors had cultivated for generations.

Arab Migration and Settlement:

Some historians argue that the economic development in Palestine, driven partly by Jewish immigration and capital, attracted Arab immigrants from neighboring regions. This is a point of contention, but evidence suggests that migration from nearby Arab areas did occur, contributing to the demographic landscape.

Bedouin Sedentarization:

The Ottoman authorities often tried to settle the nomadic Bedouin tribes to transform them into tax-paying farmers. Over time, many Bedouins became semi-sedentary, especially in the Negev region.

Infrastructural Development:

The late 19th and early 20th centuries saw significant infrastructural developments, like the Hejaz Railway. Such projects not only improved connectivity but also provided employment opportunities, attracting workers from various parts of the empire.

End of the Ottoman Era:
The fall of the Ottoman Empire after World War I led to the British taking control of Palestine under the League of Nations' mandate system. The subsequent British policies, combined with the Zionist movement and regional geopolitics, significantly influenced the demographic and political realities of modern Palestine.

BINDING OATH

The descendants of Noah, having witnessed the unimaginable scale of the great flood and the subsequent promise of rebirth, bore the profound responsibility of upholding a divine covenant. This covenant, not merely a pact with Noah but with every living creature, was symbolized by the vivid hues of the rainbow that grace our skies after rain – a visual testament to the eternal promise made by the Creator.

As these descendants ventured across the breadth of the Earth, establishing civilizations and delineating territories, they recognized the necessity of not only adhering to the divisions granted to them but also of preserving the essence of their shared legacy. In a solemn assembly, under the watchful eyes of the eldest among them, they bound themselves to an oath. This wasn't merely a casual commitment; it was a profound promise to respect the sanctity of the land, to honor the divine covenant, and to cherish their shared beginnings forever. As they raised their hands to the heavens, they resoundingly declared, "So be it," etching this oath into the annals of time. Meant to endure through the ages, this pledge wasn't just for them but for every future generation that would inherit the Earth.

Yet, as time passed, while the symbol of the covenant – the rainbow – remains ever-present, a testament to God's promise, the essence of the oath has, unfortunately, faded in most memories. The challenges and complexities of modern geopolitics and historical intricacies have overshadowed this ancient promise. It serves as a poignant reminder for all – to not only admire the beauty of the rainbow but also to remember and uphold the weight of the oath it represents.

Generations came and went, and the world evolved in ways unimaginable to those first descendants of Noah. Territories were established, civilizations rose and fell, and the once-clear waters of unity began to muddy with the sands of time.

Fast forward to today, where the echoes of that ancient oath reverberate in the heart of the Middle East. The land, steeped in history and faith, witnesses a strife that is more than territorial. The Israeli-Palestinian conflict is not just a geopolitical dispute; it's a heartbreaking testament to forgotten promises and shared legacies.

"Dividing the Earth: Noah's Legacy" is a mirror to our times, reflecting the complexities of shared histories and the pain of division. The binding oath, the eternal promise, and the declaration of "So be it" are not mere relics of the past. They are living reminders of the oath we once took, urging us to look beyond borders and honor our shared commitment.

The ancient oath, with its profound emphasis on honoring divinely ordained territories, sheds light on the deep-seated convictions held by many today. For the descendants of Noah, the land divisions were clear-cut and inviolable, each portion divinely allotted. As they proclaimed, "So be it," they not only accepted the territories given to them but also acknowledged the sanctity of those given to others.

Fast forward to today, the Israeli-Palestinian conflict is a testament to how deviations from these ancient allotments and the nuances of time have complicated matters. While the oath taken by Noah's descendants speaks of clear divisions, modern geopolitics, and historical events have blurred these boundaries. This complexity doesn't undermine the oath's significance but heightens the need for mutual understanding and dialogue.

Given the intricate weave of history and faith in the region, one possible path toward peace is recognizing and respecting the ancient divisions while acknowledging the lived realities of the present. For true reconciliation, it's crucial to honor the past and its binding promises but also to understand and address the pains, aspirations, and realities of today.

As we grapple with the intricacies of today's world, it's imperative to seek guidance from the annals of history, recognizing that the resolutions to our modern dilemmas may well be anchored in the solemn vows of those who came before us. Their unbreakable oath, taken ages ago, was a pledge to the present and the future. As custodians of this legacy, we are bound by duty and destiny to revere and realize its essence. In our actions and words, the affirmation "So be it" should not just echo as an ancient agreement but as an enduring commitment—a beacon of unity and the unyielding bond that connects generations past, present, and future.

REFLECTIONS

Reflecting upon the annals of history, one cannot help but feel a profound sympathy for the generations that have come to bear the weight of an oath they never personally took. It's especially heartrending for the Palestinian people, who find themselves in the throes of a conflict, often without fully grasping its historical roots. Their daily struggles, dreams, and aspirations are overshadowed by a pact made ages ago. It's a poignant reminder of how the choices of the past can continue to shape the destinies of people many generations later. For them, the oath is not just a historical footnote but a living testament that influences them daily. As we navigate the complexities of today's world, it's essential to acknowledge and empathize with those who bear the burdens of history, hoping for a future where understanding and compassion lead the way.

My heart deeply aches for the Palestinian people. They have become emblematic of a generation bearing the heavy chains of decisions made in a distant past, often without a comprehensive understanding of the oath's origins that now shadows their lives. The complexity of their daily experiences, where hopes, dreams, and the longing for peace clash with historical edicts, cannot be understated. The legacy of the brothers' oath, however ancient and solemn, continues to reverberate through time, touching lives and shaping destinies. But even as we empathize with the struggles of the Palestinian people, the weight and sanctity of that oath remain undiminished. The challenge for the present generation is to navigate this intricate tapestry of historical commitments and contemporary aspirations, searching for a path that honors the past while paving the way for a harmonious future.

The Oath Still Stands

BIBLIOGRAPHY

Noha, M. (1840). *The Book of Jasper*. NewYork: Facsimile Publisher.

Johnson, K. (1917). *The Ancient Book of Jublies*.

Kennedy, H. (2004). *The Prophet and the Age of the Caliphates: The Islamic Near East from the 6th to the 11th Century. Harlow: Pearson Education. (This book provides insight into the territorial delineations and nomenclature during the periods of the Umay*.

Khalidi, R. (2006). *The Iron Cage: The Story of the Palestinian Struggle for Statehood. (This book delves into the history of Palestine during the 20th century, including the period of British Mandate*. Boston: Beacon Press.

Finkelstein, I. &. ((2001).). *The Bible Unearthed: Archaeology's New Vision of Ancient Israel and the Origin of Its Sacred Texts. New York:* The Free Press.

Tubb, J. (1998)). *Canaanites*. University of Oklahoma Press.

Finkelstein, I. &. (2001). *The Bible Unearthed: Archaeology's New Vision of Ancient Israel and the Origin of Its Sacred Texts*. Free Press.

Armstrong, K. (1997). *Jerusalem: One City, Three Faiths*. Ballantine Books.

Bright, J. (2000). *A History of Israel*. Westminster John Knox Press.

Morris, B. (2008). *1948: A History of the First Arab-Israeli War*. Yale University Press.

Gelvin, J. L. (2005). *The Israel-Palestine Conflict: One Hundred Years of War*. Cambridge University Press.

Briant, P. (n.d.). *Cyrus to Alexander: A History of the Persian Empire*.

Josephus, F. (n.d.). *The Jewish War*.

Powell, L. (n.d.). *The Bar Kokhba War AD 132–135: The last Jewish revolt against Imperial Rome*.

---

i   The Holy Bible. (2 Kings 24-25, 2 Chronicles 36, Jeremiah 39-52)

ii   A pogrom is a violent riot incited with the aim of massacring or expelling an ethnic or religious group, particularly Jews